MW00435892

TADPOLE TALES

Tadpole Tales

Teaching Children
Reading and
Journal Writing

MARGARET B. KING

Story Line Press
2003

© 2003 by Margaret B. King
First Printing

All rights reserved. No part of this book may be reproduced in any form or by any electronic or mechanical means including information storage and retrieval systems without permission in writing from the publisher, except by a reviewer.

Published by Story Line Press, Three Oaks Farm, PO Box 1240, Ashland, OR 97520-0055, www.storylinepress.com.

This publication was made possible thanks in part to the generous support of the Nicholas Roerich Museum, the Andrew W. Mellon Foundation and our individual contributors.

Cover art by Margaret B. King
Book design by Sharon McCann

Library of Congress Cataloging-in-Publication Data

King, Margaret B., 1947–
Tadpole tales : teaching children reading and journal writing / by Margaret B. King.
p. cm.
ISBN 1-58654-026-2
1. Reading (Early childhood) 2. Diaries—Authorship.
3. Children—Books and reading. I. Title.
LB1139.5.R43 K56 2003
372.4—dc21

2002154851

For Maxine and Shelley,
my two best teachers

Contents

Foreword

" **T**eaching children to read is much like teaching birds to fly," Margaret King informs us, opening her first chapter on "Reading, that Mysterious Process" with this analogy. If anyone pondering this imponderable has teased apart its mystery, it is she.

Over years as a teacher of pre-kindergarten and kindergarten children, King has developed a story-telling method that stimulates youngsters to recreate elements of the plot pictorially. When they ask for a word to describe the picture, she supplies it. The older children, who have already acquired the alphabet, are encouraged to copy the word. The younger pre-literates are encouraged to stay in their seats, to color the shapes they have made. The important thing is "to get them to value the piece of paper in front of them, and to see it as an exciting possibility for their ideas."

This is not a revolutionary concept. But King possesses a heightened intuition on the job. Because she loves what she does, she does it well, as ensuing chapters attest. In "Color as Categorization," King discusses the emotional power of color. For instance, in a story about a dragon who breathes fire, "All the children used the red pens for the fire and the eyes. . . . It gave them the idea that words and pictures are symbols of this higher excitement of the mind."

King is disarmingly straightforward in her exposition. But for the reader who wants a more scientific overview, she restates: "A foundation in drawing and coloring on the preschool level trains the brain in spatial and logical procedure.... It also stimulates the imagination in that emotive intensity connected with art which spurs the activity of reading.... Most of all, learning to draw and color facilitates those decision-making qualities that seek to isolate and categorize, making it possible to read." Being a fine artist, King should know!

When it comes to selecting stories appropriate for retelling, stories that will keep little kids in their seats, King takes an eclectic approach. The goal is to choose stories that generate excitement. "This," she says, "can only be done if the teacher is excited, and takes the story to heart by rehearsing it ahead of time, usually at home where there is no pressure to perform." Alas, rehearsing ahead of time probably eliminates a large proportion of nursery–school teachers.

Folk tales, fairy tales, stories from history are rich resources. I was pleased to discover King's inclusion of tales from Greek mythology: "The great tales spun through the ages to explain the concepts closest to the human heart are still very much a force in teaching little children to read." These have to be abbreviated and much of the dark side expurgated, but King has had great success, for example, with the story of King Midas.

A chapter on discipline precedes the final section, the tales themselves. The Dreikurs model and the Frederic H. Jones model provide the unsure teacher with positive reinforcement in dealing with attention getting, power seeking, and so on. The correct use of body language, the use of an incentive system, and the security of structure are all discussed, along with Margaret King's earthy, commonsensical advice: "How was my entrance? Did I greet them positively and with joy?... Did I make sure they all had their shoes on and tied?"

Lucky, lucky kids with their shoes on and tied! And lucky readers, who will be encouraged, greeted positively and with joy, not preached at but helped to be better, more creative teachers, who rehearse at home and come to class brimful of enthusiasm, with scads of fresh paper and tons of crayons.

—*Maxine Kumin*

Introduction

Tadpole Tales is a guide and method of teaching preschool children the basic reading skills they will develop in first grade. Preschool children as young as four years old have an amazing aptitude to learn. They are easily stimulated by the creative process of word–picture association coupled with telling stories in the oral tradition using dialogue.

My method of teaching employs journal writing in the context of creative dialogue between teacher and children. I explain to my students that their primary goal is to learn to read, and secondarily to write, and that reading and writing are one. When met by puzzled stares, I explain by using the example of how we talk with tongue and breath: "You cannot sound out words by using the tongue alone, nor by using the breath alone. To make words that we can hear, you need to use both your breath and your tongue, and the result is talking! In my journal class, you will learn both reading and writing together as you first listen to my story and then create your own stories."

Through journal writing, preschool children aged four to five years are introduced to the use of words as symbols of meaning, and they are empowered to use these symbols. Children in kindergarten aged five and six years, who already know how to write letters, use journal writing to learn how to write complete sentences. These children are challenged and encouraged on the path to literacy by drawing and coloring.

This method is a simple and direct way of teaching children how to listen, conceptualize and form words while developing the fine-motor skills of writing and drawing. The method evolved over seven years with much trial and error and always a "go with the flow" approach to see which stories are most effective and how to use an exciting delivery.

"Give me a word!" is the cry my students make when they are ready to attach the mysterious element of writing to their pictures. So I give them words that they will learn to use later on when they can read in first grade. One of my graduates started writing a book in second grade—a total of nine pages of an exciting story according to his parent—thanks to my teaching method. Such positive results can make a big difference in the life of a child.

The core of the journal approach revolves around telling exciting, dramatic stories with good humor and values (possibly with conflict between good and evil scaled to a child's understanding), opening doors to a child's questing mind. Children readily soak up new ideas, especially between two and six years—there is no age as keen and perceptive.

It is crucial to the success of the journal approach that teachers learn how to tell—not read—a story. Active storytelling puts the teacher in immediate and vital touch with his or her students. Any teacher can learn to tell a story. All it requires is enthusiasm, a certain amount of rehearsal, and a confident and dramatic presentation. Once the children focus with full attention on the storyteller, it becomes easy to teach. There is no headier wine for teachers than attentive and interested pupils who look forward to instruction the next day. *Tadpole Tales* presents the ways and means of effective storytelling and the kinds of stories to be used.

The teacher may wish to tell stories with the help of visual aids. Drawing simple contour or line images on the chalkboard enhances student concentration while the stories are told. The teacher must explain that the children need not copy such a drawing but use the image as ideas for pictures of their own. The point of a visual aid is to stimulate the imagination; therefore, the teacher's images should be simple but lively. The teacher adds impact to the story by changing or adding to the visual aid as the story progresses, which demonstrates to the children that they have the power to create their own world, a world of symbol and meaning.

Tadpole Tales is divided in three parts. Part one is an overview of the mysterious process of how young children investigate the tools and symbols of basic reading, not through phonics or phonemes based on the alphabet, but through pictures as ideas that translate into words and sentences, that is, units of meaning. The strength of this method results from the creative input of the children themselves who seize hold of the ideas presented in the story and go on to produce their own visual concepts by coloring and then by defining their ideas by words. By journal writing, drawing and coloring, they learn to give voice to their most significant moments of enthusiasm. Because they invest so much of themselves in the process, they learn how words are the basic units of meaning.

Also in part one, chapter five, are tips on storytelling. When telling stories, a good sense of humor is crucial because children often find funny what the teacher may not. In the end, it is the teacher's own enthusiasm for the story that inspires excellence in the classroom. Chapter six reviews the sources of where to find stories, for there is a wealth of stories from mythology, science, math, history, and fantasy within reach of the teacher who seeks them.

Part two presents fourteen stories chosen from more than a hundred simple tales to which my students have responded with enthusiasm—stories to which they can relate such as birthdays (very important to a young child), adventures in which they can possibly take part, and themes that spark curiosity about the everyday world.

17

Part three explains the rewarding process of making a book from the child's journal. The emotional impact on children of book making is enormous. Parents have told me that their children have slept with them under their pillows. Once at rest time I discovered a little boy sleeping with his book clutched in his hand!

I hope that the methods presented in *Tadpole Tales* will ignite the imagination of preschool teachers and students alike. By encouraging the development of fine motor skills and picture–word associations through storytelling, children learn to read and write by phonics or the system based on phonemes by Diane McGuiness, presented in her book *Why Our Children Can't Read And What We Can Do About It*. If the methods in *Tadpole Takes* are followed, preschool children will be well prepared for achieving literacy later on.

I am indebted to educators who have contributed much to the field of early childhood education. I utilize the ideas of Jean Piaget for assimilation, Vygotsky for scaffolding, the Dreikers and Jones models for discipline, and Atkinson–Shiffrin for the learning model based on how a computer remembers and how it might relate to a child's mind. I thank Mary Reck Jalongo for permission to use information from her article, "Teaching Children to Become Better Listeners," published by the National Association for the Education of Young Children. I am grateful for C.M. Charles' excellent book, *Building Classroom Discipline*, and thank Random House for allowing me to use Isak Dinesen's quotations from *Last Tales* on the power of words.

PART ONE

Teaching and Learning
As Creative Dialogue

1. Reading, that Mysterious Process

Teaching children to read is much like teaching birds to fly. Once I watched barn swallow fledglings launch themselves into space. Uncertain at first of the vocabulary of wind and air speed, they gradually grew accustomed to the movement of their wings as useful tools for lofting them over the lake and into the blue sky. Then, imitating their parents, they skimmed over the water, dive-bombed insects, and negotiated the difficult landing procedure. How they learned all these things is innate, mysterious.

Children undergo the same mystical process when learning to read. For a long time, they are spoon-fed the letters of the alphabet and the verbal phonetics linking letters to sound. Suddenly they begin to associate words with the pictures in their own minds or on paper. They string together phrases, and by repetition, gain an insight into inflection and types of sentences. One day, perhaps by laboriously sounding out syllables and letters, they suddenly begin to read, just as the swallows took flight. But how this process works is an imponderable. We can only guess at some of it.

My purpose as a teacher of journal writing to pre-kindergarten and kindergarten students was to get them to turn their ideas into images, and create symbols that express these ideas—symbols that are words. I discovered that a strong story told orally with images drawn on the chalkboard was a sure stimulus to learning how to associate pictures with words to prepare the mind to read. I was not so interested in the reading process as I was in preparing the groundwork for reading by helping children understand that words are strong vehicles of imagination, and that imagination means power—for a start, the power to communicate a fantastic or wonderful experience. The telling of the story was the driving force that pushed these little swallows over the edge of their nests and launched them into flight.

Stories predate writing by thousands of years. Through stories, myth, tradition, religion, and history, a wealth of culture was handed down from elders of the tribe. In the modern preschool classroom, little children look to the teacher much as the tribal young looked to their elders for the secrets of the universe and the knowledge of survival. Little children have faith in their teachers. It is wise to give them only the best stories, purged of excessive violence, but with a strong plot, presenting heroes and villains engaged in the struggle between good and evil. The story must be told with simple concepts and words to make it interesting to young children and to stimulate them to translate the ideas into pictures.

My method was to tell the story with vigor and spirit. Using simple images, I drew on the chalkboard to enhance high points. Then I required the children to draw something that related to the story and color it. They would next ask me for a word, or words, which described their picture. I would print carefully the word(s) on a tent-shaped piece of cardboard and place it in front of them and they would copy it. The teaching of writing in this way presupposed an acquaintance with the letters of the alphabet, upper and lower case, which the five-year-olds had already learned. The four-year-olds who were admitted to my journal class were of mixed ability. In the first years I took them all, but more recently only the most advanced of their group were admitted, those who had already mastered the skills needed to write in upper and lower case.

I want to stress that it was the process, not the product, that occupied their attention. We worked on a new journal page every day. Frequently they "messed up" and would want to start over again, but I encouraged them to "fix it" on the same piece of paper. I wanted to give them a sense of doing the work as a project with a beginning, a middle, and an end that needed to be completed within a certain time period (usually 45 minutes). I wanted to give them a sense of continuity, of scaffolding. Every day they were building on the work of the day before and improving on it. And finally, I wanted these free-flying swallows to delight in the final product—a book, a book of their own journal pages neatly stapled together within a cover of their own making. We spent a whole session on making these covers as wonderful and exciting as possible, using pens, markers, crayons, and finally an orgy of stickers. All preschool children love stickers, so these made their work particularly special. Now, they could present their books of journal writing to their parents.

Parental involvement is crucial to learning, particularly in the lower grades and preschool. Inside the cover of each journal book I stapled a letter to parents explaining how the journal works. (Sample letters are included in the appendix.) I hoped for parents to look over the books and exclaim with interest and enthusiasm, giving their children a sense of the importance of words and a confidence with writing that would carry through in all their subsequent work in school. There is no prize in the world as great as the heady enjoyment of pleasing a parent. To make it easier for the parents to understand, I always wrote the title of the story at the bottom of each journal page and the date of the particular page at the top, so the parents could see how their children were progressing.

I want to point out that my journal teaching was not the one-on-one experience with each child that parents often practice when reading stories at bedtime. The nightly story is, in the greatest sense, a powerful impetus to read. I taught a group and needed to discipline. I discovered through trial and error that the best means of discipline was foresight. On the first day I talked with the children and announced the rules for my class. They were to put on their shoes (after rest) and quietly find their seats at the journal tables without boisterous talking or disruptive behavior. They were to listen attentively to the story ("One, two, three, all eyes on me!") without making rude sounds or interjecting questions—there would be time for questions at the end. They were to receive the paper and pencil or pen handed out to them and start right to work on their drawing. They were never, under any circumstances, to make fun of another child's drawing or to draw on another's paper. Even wanting to "help" was limited to drawing on a separate piece of cardboard or paper. They were to proceed from drawing, to coloring, to word writing with a minimum of fuss and within the time limit. Finally, they would answer four questions by which they would know the project was at an end to give a sense of closure. The four questions are: (1) Did you draw a picture? (2) Did you color the picture? (3) Did you write a word, or words? (4) Did you write your name? This class management was the result of many years teaching experience, and I found it worked very well to set limits and let children know what was expected of them right at the beginning.

It must be understood that every group is different and poses particular problems that cannot be covered by a panacea of discipline skills, but must be directed specifically to the needs of the group. For instance, one year I had a group with a large number of four-year-olds who simply could not keep up with the five-year-olds. I had to deal with them on an individual "spoon-feeding" basis.

Another year, I had a group of boisterous boys who enjoyed stories of rocket ships and Ninjas. This was a "gender typing" issue, for try as many educators do, they cannot wholly eradicate the profound biological differences between little girls and little boys. On a preschool level these are manifested by the culturally conditioned, masculine models for boys, such as matchbox cars, fighter action figures, Batman heroes and the like. These are in contrast to the girls' gentler maternal images of dolls, Barbies, and elements of adornment, such as hair ribbons, that create what I call "the princess identity."

Another year, I had a group composed mostly of girls with only three boys in it. They evolved into a party group, given to laughing at everything, funny or not, singing popular tunes, and gossiping with heightened interest about the few boys in the class. This was clearly a social issue as the children attempted to define their roles and personalities in relationship to peers, an activity which took precedence over much of what the teacher was saying. The most rigid discipline was necessary to direct this group's attention both to the story and to the completion of their work within the allotted time. They were children with excellent potential but who needed rigorous guidance to bring it out in them. Naturally, I had to handle the boisterous boys in a different manner from the party group of gossiping girls. These children presented a challenge to my teaching skills, which I embraced wholly, utilizing firmness and a good sense of humor.

Most recently I have what looks like a model journal group of eight to ten members, not the larger twelve to fourteen members of past years. They all listen attentively and work assiduously, but tend to be perfectionists who spend half their time erasing what they have already drawn and taking the full time to finish. They lack a certain spontaneity seen in the earlier groups.

The fascinating interplay between group personality and the teacher is a challenging aspect of teaching journal writing, or any kind of teaching. One must be aware of the discipline strategies taught in various books on preschool education, such as the ripple effect, scaffolding, and judicious praise given to one of the group as a good example so the others might imitate but not copy, and wise use of incentives, such as stickers presented occasionally for work well done.

I would like to discuss in anecdotal format some of the challenges and problems I have encountered while teaching journal class to four- and five-year-olds, with a view to laying the groundwork for their learning to read in the first grade. These are pre-literate children. To them every letter is a mysterious symbol that must be mastered by an almost Berlitz method of saturation. They must keep seeing a particular letter and experiencing it, hear the sound it makes over and over, and they must draw the letter again and again with pencil, with crayon, in the sand, in the dirt with a stick, and if possible even cut out its shape. Gradually, knowledge of the letter will "sink in." The mysterious process of learning that symbols can be put together to form words will take place; and gradually the understanding of how these words can be strung together to form phrases, and then sentences, and whole blocks of meaning will be unlocked to them. They will learn to read. Books and computers will be open to them. The whole wonderful process starts at the pre-literate level of picture associated with story, represented by words.

I begin in September by telling very simple tales of exposition. What is the perfect food? I draw and discuss vegetables and fruit and meat, and finally the cow and her milk.

Such simple stories appeal to very young journal writers, the four-year-olds. Johnny, for example, just turned four and still acts like a "hyper" three-year-old. Michael can hardly hold a pencil and scribbles instead of draws. Neither of them can write any letters except, perhaps, the first letter of their names. My main struggle is to persuade them to stay in their seats. But I know and have confidence that teaching journaling is developmental and progressive. Once they settle into the task at hand they will scaffold, or build upon disciplined habits of the day before, especially if I work with them every day, showing them how to hold their pencil, reminding them to stay in their seats, and encouraging them to color the shapes they have made on the paper. For these young ones, it is important to get them to value the piece of paper in front of them and to see it as an exciting possibility for their ideas. I teach them to resist the urge to crumple it up or to start over. Gradually these two boys became proficient in the art of drawing and writing, although it took many months of practice.

The older ones, the five–year–olds, have already mastered their own bodies, and by successive learning sessions have understood that they must stay in their chairs and do their work. They come to my journal table already armed with a knowledge of letters, both upper and lower case. They are enthusiastic about storytelling, which is entertaining and gives them a sense of play. I urge them to turn this sense of play into hard work by conceptualizing and drawing specific themes from the story. They may imitate each other's ideas, but exact copying is discouraged. I take great pains with each of them, separately attending to their needs and wishes, and finally at the time of the four questions, give a quick, judicious review of their work. "You need to try to write on the lines," I might say, for the journal paper has a blank area at the top for draw-ing and lines at the bottom for writing. "You should try to make your letters all the same size." Or, "Don't make your let-ters dance up and down but lay them straight." I give words of praise too. "Nice coloring. You stayed in the lines and pressed hard, covering all the white spaces," I might say. Or, "You for-got to color the man's face. Try it!" Such words as "You did a terrific job today," "You did an excellent drawing today," and "You included every part of the story in your picture" are never absent from my vocabulary. But I do not praise indis-criminately. Too much praise cheapens itself into insincerity. I tell the children to look long and hard at their work, and we go over it together. When I speak, it is with a tone of sinceri-ty and quiet regulation. I want them to develop a sense of self-criticism without being overwhelmed by an impossible stan-dard of perfection. I do this by asking them to fulfill the requirements of the project. If they do more, such as adding themes to their drawings that they "thought up themselves" or coming up with unusual words to put with their pictures, then I let them know they have done exceptionally well by striking out into the unknown.

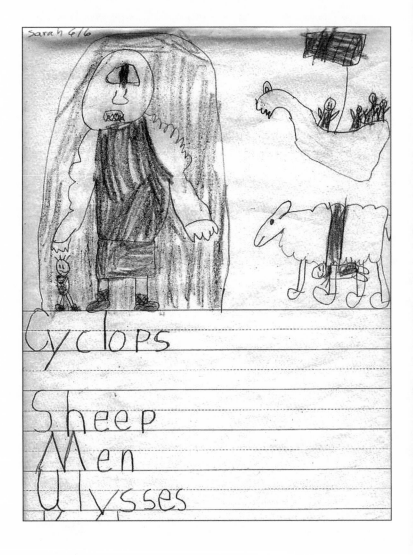

2. How Children Suddenly "Get It"

I shall begin this chapter by discussing the drawing component of journal writing because it is by drawing that the seeds of ideas are implanted in a child's mind. "I think, and then I draw my think" is a succinct way of describing the process that is the first step toward reading what others think. When a child approaches the awesome task of trying to get his idea down on paper, he must concentrate on the complex but logically interwoven ideas that the teacher marshals to make a story. This is order, not chaos. It imposes a discipline of the mind in which excitement, fun, or even the hint of danger are used to elevate the imagination.

A child is not interested in making a pretty picture. Nor is he or she interested in setting down advanced art concepts such as perspective and shading. He only knows that when he hears an exciting thought he is to respond by putting it down on paper. In this way, the story becomes almost like magic, and the children draw what is most important to them thematically. Often they draw one thing looming large in the middle of the page. Sometimes they draw small things in a row at the bottom of the page or scattered about as if floating in space. They have no idea of spatial organization or scale at age four. By the time they are six, they have subconsciously imbibed these ideas and may incorporate them into their pictures, but in the beginning they are only interested in putting down the main theme.

It is amazing the difference between what a child six years of age can do compared to a child of four years, and yet it must be remembered that the groundwork is laid at the earlier age. A baby must crawl before it can walk. The experts say that if a baby is not allowed to crawl, she misses an important perceptual discovery period in her development; and so it is with conceptualizing. What a four–year–old draws may often look like a scribble or unrelated tangles of lines until she starts using universal shapes such as the circle. But if this important stage in the drawing–life of a child is missed, she may lack spatial organization in her thought patterns and suffer in future attempts at subjects such as math and science. This is why drawing is so important, even if the shapes drawn are not recognizable to adult eyes.

The apparently "primitive" scribbles are early steps in the development of a much more complicated process that is slowly taking place in the mind of the child. Daily repetition of the practice of drawing is necessary if children are to learn to give form to ideas. They require repeated exposure to the thought–organizing techniques the teacher employs to tell a story before they are able to grasp salient points and make drawings out of them. The freshness and spontaneity of each child's drawing should be emphasized and encouraged, for the first struggles to draw are monumental; they release the child's ability to pour out emotions and ideas onto paper. No matter how small, disorganized, or scribbled the "picture" is, the teacher must understand that it is a process going on within the child's mind; and the product, at this stage, is far less important than the child's ongoing excitement and willingness to produce. Process is more desirable than product and it is up to the teacher to keep this flame alive. With daily practice the drawings will improve and become tangible expressions of ideas. This process leads to reading.

Halfway through the school year, I found it useful to restate the purpose and reason behind journal teaching. The children were well acquainted with the four step process of listening, drawing, coloring, and writing words, but they had forgotten why they were doing it. So I asked them, "Why do you think you are doing journal writing?" Several raised their hands, but only a few gave me the correct answer: "So that we can learn to read." And I asked them, "Do you know why I draw pictures on the chalkboard? I draw them so that you will see the word that is written under them. Sometimes the word will say exactly what you think the picture is, and sometimes it will surprise you and teach you something new."

Then I told the story of how the kangaroo got its long legs. In this folk tale, Kangaroo boasts of being the fastest animal in the world, and has to outrun a wild dingo with many teeth. On the chalkboard, I drew Kangaroo without long legs, then with long legs. I also drew the toothy dingo, a cactus, the hot sun, and a round circle representing a pool of water. The words "sun," "cactus" and "kangaroo" they understood. The word "dingo" they did not, so I had to explain that it was the wild dog of Australia. The pool of water, I said, was a "billabong" or swamp. Big snakes live in the sand and mud all around it. Kangaroo got away from the dingo by plunging into the billabong, and then a big snake scared him off. Thus, I showed them that words can have the exact meaning of what the picture looks like, but can also give them new meanings, such as "dingo" and "billabong."

The following examples demonstrate how children can progress. In each case I describe the symbols the child used, and the length of time it took before he or she began to produce drawings that related to the story.

Rianna started my journal class when she was four and responded in the same manner to all the stories. No matter what themes or subjects were discussed, she always drew pictures of her mom. Sometimes she would enlarge on the concept by drawing her mom and herself. These symbols were round circles for faces and straight bodies having no arms or

31

legs. They were always smiling. She used vivid colors to accentuate her pictures. When she became five, she exploded with new ideas. She stopped drawing pictures of her mom and began drawing unicorns, butterflies, or vegetables—whatever the story was about. She needed an entire year of drawing nothing but mom, who was the most important part of her life, before she could draw anything else. I always complemented her drawings and never criticized her or tried to force her to change subject matter. I knew that eventually she would begin to perceive the world with a larger perspective.

The girl from Spain only wanted to draw the sun. Sun symbols are universal for children throughout the world and particularly for this girl who had lived in sunny Spain. She always drew it in the upper left hand corner, and only after much encouragement did she begin to draw themes from the story, first very small, and then amplifying them. This girl was already five years old and utilized the idea of a ground line in her pictures. Sky and sun were above; earth and grass were below. Figures walked on the grass. She caught on very quickly, and within two months her pictures were full of thematic ideas. But she still would draw the sun before anything else.

Nathan, a five-year-old, was so enthusiastic about drawing that he bubbled over and couldn't wait to start. No matter what the story was about, he always drew specter-like figures with big round circles for heads and straight bodies having no arms or legs. But he put different expressions on their faces, which showed an unusual awareness of emotive force. Most children, if happy and well-adjusted, always draw their people smiling. Nathan tried to make his characters take on the emotion of the story. I could see the process evolving within his active imagination and knew that he was one who would quickly catch on to larger themes. At the beginning however, the drawing of figures was what released the inner fire of his imagination.

A boy named Chris had a scientific approach to drawing.

He would attempt to put down salient themes from the story, all in small pictures on the paper, loosely at first, and later in connected contexts. He manifested cataloging tendencies by drawing each item that interested him as though he were making an inventory. At first these items were hanging in free space on the page, but as the class continued, day by day, they began to attain a new continuity that reflected a linking of thought patterns. He was four when he started. By age five he was drawing magnificently recognizable pictures, and his themes were united and organized.

Two scribblers, Matt and Mike, simply could not think of anything to draw and made large or tight, angry scribbles on the page. These two were challenging because they seemed so blocked. I suggested they make simple shapes, like a circle repeated over and over again, or a square, or just parallel lines—anything that would establish that they were organizing their ideas onto the page. Matt went away for a year and then came back. He had been a scribbler at age four, but when he returned to journal class, he suddenly could draw. A variety of themes poured out from his pencil. This shows what a difference a year can make.

Mike scribbled because he did not care. Nothing seemed to interest him except interaction with his peers. One day during rest period when all the other journal writers were still asleep, he suddenly got it. I told him the story of the brown rabbit who nearly gets caught by a fox before he changes his color to white and is able to hide in the snow. Mike could concentrate because he was not performing for his peers, and he began to draw. He suddenly drew the rabbit. Such a breakthrough as this points out an important fact—preschoolers have the ability to listen attentively and focus on the story. A teacher should never give up on them, no matter how disruptive some of them may behave in a group situation. One good day can change the behavior of a journal writer from mediocre to excellent, and once the advantage has been gained, it should be pressed to the fullest. I was careful to lavish praise on Mike, and in subsequent journal classes I reminded him how well he had done the day he drew the rabbit. Ever afterward, he would always draw at least one theme from the story.

Another child, Fred, was extremely bright but inexperienced with drawing. He kept interrupting the story with questions until I politely told him to have good manners and that I would explain it to him later. Once the story was over, I said, "That's your story for today, now let's draw!" I passed out the paper and the pencils and waited a few minutes so the children could have time to think about it. After a suitable pause, when all had begun drawing, I circled around to Fred who was climbing on his chair and falling off of it. I explained to him that if he wanted to do a good job of journal writing, he had to sit with his bottom on the chair and his feet dangling down to face the table. (Posture is of the essence in any writing or drawing exercise. It must be learned at a young age or the child will have problems later on.) Fred straightened himself out and kept asking his questions. I answered each of them and then suggested he draw something. He tried to draw everything on the chalkboard and ended up with a mass of scribbles. He was a late four–year–old turning five, and had had no previous practice. I suggested he draw the world. I showed him on a piece of cardboard how the United States of America was at the top of the world and Australia was at the bottom. My drawing looked like a round baseball. But he grasped the concept of the world and was quickly able to draw it on his own paper. Then I asked him to color it. Again, he was uncertain how to start, so I showed him by making repetitive sweeping motions of the crayon, staying within the outline of the world drawn on my little cardboard. I used two different colors, one to represent the ocean and one to represent land. This kind of representational categorization was totally new to him, since he was "color illiterate," but he did it and was proud of it. It was one of his first journal pages, and it was, for him, a positive experience. Instead of being frustrated and not able to draw as all the other children around him were doing, he was allowed to find his own level and put something down on the page, which he would ever after recognize as "the world."

Some children have the problem of being perfectionists; that is, they have a grandiose concept in their minds that they seek to put down on paper, and when it turns out wrong, they get frustrated and erase it. Some have even crumpled their papers up and tried to throw them away, but I judiciously saved them at the last minute. I uncrumple the page, put it in front of the child and say, "Now then. What's so awful about this picture?" The child will say, "It doesn't look like a dragon." And I say, "Yes it does. It's a very good dragon. You must never throw away your drawings. Try again." I have the child turn over the page, and draw the image again. If he or she is still frustrated with the drawing, I provide a new sheet of paper but explain that each drawing he did was worthy. "Everybody draws in a different way," I say. "Now, let me show you." And on a separate piece of cardboard I make a drawing composed of circles, rectangles, and triangles to indicate the basic shapes. But most of the time I say, "Look at the board. You can get out of your seat and go look at the drawings on the board, and see how to draw it."

Once a boy named David started a wonderful drawing of a dog. It looked just like a sophisticated artist's cartoon for the local newspaper, but it didn't live up to his expectations and he was about to throw it away. I rescued it and said, "This will be your first drawing, David. Now try a second sheet of paper. I will keep this first drawing to put in your final journal book along with the second one you are doing." He was willing to accept this and put them both in his final book. David drew like an engineer with connected causality. I told him that his drawings were like an engineer's because they showed how things work. He wanted to know what an engineer was. "An engineer is someone who builds bridges, or rocket ships, or laser machines in outer space. You keep drawing, and maybe some day you will be an engineer." He was full of enthusiasm. "Neat!" he said and continued to draw with precision and to make meaningful themes. He was five and a half, and though he began to journal in September not really knowing what it was all about, the ideas soon poured from his pencil.

A few words about materials. I like to start my class using pencils. I buy festive ones with designs, such as suns, fishes, or fireworks. Once at Halloween, I got "Monster" pencils with pictures of the Mummy, Frankenstein and Dracula. At Christmas time, I favor red and green "Season's Greetings" pencils. The pencils should be special. They should signal to the children "Now it's time to start drawing. Here I am! Your journal pencil!"

The first year, I used plain four-inch pencils with no erasers. This did not work well. It did not give the children that special journal feeling, and they could not erase. Even though I discourage erasing, I allow them to do it with the cautionary warning, "The first thing that comes from your pencil is the best thing." But if they feel they have to erase, they may choose to do so. To vary their writing materials I also give them colored pens in green, pink, yellow, and purple, or on a certain day (such as Valentine's Day, or after a brave adventure story of dragon killing), all red pens. I also give them colorful pens that write with black ink. The fun of using colored pens is very great, but regardless of ink color, it is an important choice for them to make since I explain that they cannot erase the marks made by pen. If they choose to use pen despite this warning, it shows a terrific confidence in their own drawing skill that is much to be desired. Confidence in approaching the page is a trait that helps them greatly in first grade.

For paper, I use large quantities of manila paper that is ruled at the bottom but has a large empty rectangle at the top for drawing. It shows at a glance the interpenetration of ideas represented in drawing and in writing. One's eye goes back and forth with immediacy between the top and the bottom, interpreting the pictures and matching the pictures with the words. I explain to the children that paper is valuable and should not be wasted. It is especially valuable once they have made their mark on it, for then it is an expression of self. "Now it is yours!" I tell them.

After they have drawn the picture, they are asked to color it. For this, I purchase Crayola crayons in quantity; I find they are the strongest and most diverse in color. Each box of crayons is placed in a plastic "boat," not left in the box so that the boys and girls can see the colors set out. Also, this eliminates the problem of cleaning up the crayons; they can be tossed back into the plastic boat. At preschool, time is valuable, and we operate on a very tight schedule; precious minutes for cleaning up are not to be had. Twenty-four crayons may sound like a lot, but more than one shade of blue is a challenge to their color literacy, which I discuss in the next chapter.

As an alternative to crayons, it is also fun to vary color materials once in a while with markers. But they are not as desirable because they tend to soak through the paper and not give the children a crisp line.

Props are useful to add excitement to the story. If it is about "Lady Bug, Lady Bug, Fly Away Home" (your house is on fire, your children are alone, so call 911), I use a small matchbox model of a fire truck, which I pass around the table so the children can see and touch it. Once I brought in a live baby snapping turtle in a bowl of water and told a story about it. This was met with keen excitement and was remembered long afterwards. Any prop can do, so long as it is passed around fairly and not hoarded by any one of the children. It should be placed on the table for them all to look at and examine for a few minutes, then should be removed, so that it does not become a distraction.

Paper, pencils, colored pens, crayons, markers, props are the basic materials for journal writing class. At the end of class I collect the papers and place them in a notebook. Later, I file them in each child's file folder. The date is placed at the top of every page with the title of the story at the bottom. The collection grows and grows until it becomes time for one of the quarterly books to be sent home. Covers are made out of construction paper by the children in a glory of excitement and stickers. Then I assemble the books, stapling them along the spines, insert letters describing the methods, and send them home to the parents.

3. Color as Categorization

Why is color so important? We perceive the world in terms of color. It enriches us, physically and emotionally, and feeds us spiritually by affecting our feelings to lead us to a higher emotional state. For example, the colors of spring—bright green grass, yellow daffodils and jonquils, scarlet tulips—put us in a festive mood, buoyant and hopeful. The colors of autumn—orange, crimson and brown—may be exciting but signal the end of summer and temper our expectation of delight. The colors of winter render us thoughtful: stark, black trees against white snow, and silver-gray skies make us pensive and introspective. From a practical point of view, color aids our depth perception so we can see the proximity of objects. Most important of all, it is by means of color that we categorize our world. Color and shape go together as the twin vehicles by which we perceive and differentiate objects. By teaching children the correct use of color, I am also teaching them to categorize which is a pre-reading skill.

I now refer briefly to the work of Jean Piaget, who has influenced the modern teaching methods of young children. His theory of cognition has three stages: (1) assimilation, by which the child explores and gains on knowledge of the world; (2) accommodation, by which the information is stored, so to speak, in a file cabinet of the mind; and (3) equilibrium, by which the constant energy of assimilating and accommodating are brought together to form a harmonious world view.

So it is with a child who first approaches color. The skill of using color to categorize has to be learned. Most often a child faced with a tub of twenty-four crayons will not choose a color, but will pick up one at random and begin to color. It is only by the use of judicious questioning that the "file cabinet" mentality can be enlarged to accommodate more than one color—three or more is what I ask for. I ask searching questions like "Look at the cowboy you have drawn. Is the man the same color as the horse? And what color is his skin?" I do not tell the child what color to make the man, the horse, or the skin, but I suggest that she use different colors. At first, this is difficult, but as the class meets every day, the child eventually sees that the separate objects in the picture need to be differentiated by using various colors of her own choosing. This empowers her to think clearly and selectively, thus paving the way for categorization that words will later unlock.

One of my goals is to make sure my journal writers become "color literate," that is, they use an entire vocabulary of color to categorize the different elements in their drawings. "If you have drawn it, you have to color it," I tell them, and I encourage them to color all the shapes they have made on the page.

Similarly, the fine motor skills need to be addressed in the exercise of coloring. How the children hold their crayons, whether they press down hard or soft, and how they use rhythmic motions to cover the white spaces on the page are all important. In the beginning they make disorganized scribbles that only approximate staying within the lines of the shapes they have drawn. As they become more skilled, they may learn to make wide sweeping motions back and forth and thus cover the white spaces more effectively. Some children like to bear down hard on the crayons, giving a brilliant enameled effect. I encourage them to think in terms of representation. For example, a boy named Tyler, who was of a categorizing turn of mind, asked me the exact colors of the hound in "The Fox and the Hound" story. I told him it was a Plott hound, one that had a black back and tail, but tan legs and muzzle. Tyler was satisfied with this description and went on to color his hound accordingly. He was thinking in a pre-literate sense in terms of representation and symbol. This is a pre-reading skill that enabled him to take flight later when confronted by the mystery of words.

Children react very strongly to the emotional use of color. I often hand out red pens if the theme of the story is one of love or excitement, for example, a story about a Valentine's party or a story about a dragon sweeping down from the hills breathing fire and flashing red angry eyes. Using red helps children categorize and bring out heightened excitement in their pictures and helps them understand how words and pictures are symbols of love and excitement.

When children are captivated by an idea, they want to make sure they use the correct color, according to their previous knowledge of the subject. This is called scaffolding, a principle of the Russian child psychologist, L.S. Vygotsky. Though I start with easy stories when the class begins in September, I scaffold day by day and build up to more and more complex plots and characters in my stories. The children progress with each paper they do. The story about Ninja Turtles and the Slime Monster is an excellent tool for stimulating children to think clearly about what color they will choose.

I begin this story describing the four Ninja Turtles, Leonardo, Michelangelo, Raphael, and Donatello, and how they fight crime. Then I show the bad guy, Draco (a sinister face with drooping moustaches), and explain how he used chemicals in his laboratory to create an evil slime monster, as tall as a skyscraper, that is attaching itself to buildings in New York City and disintegrating them with its slime. The Ninja Turtles bring salt guns and shoot the monster with salt so that it shrinks like a slug until nothing is left but an oily blob on the ground. Then they capture Draco and put him in jail. This colorful story gives them lots of ideas. They know the turtles are green and brown, but what color is the slime monster? It is very important for them to decide, and some say it is purple and some say it is green. I have never seen an orange or a red slime monster in their work, for the children think in terms of earth tones when confronted with this story.

Color choice is a large step in becoming color–literate, and the decision to use one color over another prepares the child to choose the right representational word. These skills flow into one another—picture–making (drawing), then color literacy, then writing representational words as symbols, then at a later date, scaffolding to yield complete sentences with a subject and predicate, a complete thought! At the early stages of journal writing, the children are encouraged to color the drawings they make because coloring is the powerful force that opens up the "file cabinets" of their minds and unlocks the wellsprings of creativity.

By the age of four, some children are already gifted with color literacy and display knowledge of the complete color spectrum when beginning to journal. Others restrict their palette to a range of colors that suits them, which they use over and over again. For example, Annie uses many colors in a harmonious way, so that her pictures look brilliant as a flower garden with vibrant complementary colors like red and green, blue and orange right next to each other. Katie uses softer colors in a rainbow effect. Brant's pictures explode with hot oranges and fiery reds and deep powerful blacks. Carl is austere in his use of browns and grays, blues and tans. Rianna uses blue in everything, for that is her favorite color at the moment, although this may change.

Using color releases strong emotional forces in these children. They become keen and eager, so that by the time they reach the journal writing step where they must put a word, or words to their picture, they have that focus and edge that enables them to think clearly and with intensity. This process is so important in the first steps to reading. The things on the page must be packed with meaning, and the symbols the children create are precisely that—packed with meaning, their own meaning, which they personally include in their own work. It is because they listened well to the story, conceptualized, emotionally made use of color, and finally, were led to a pitch of excitement to put a word to their creations that the desire to read comes alive in their minds and hearts.

As a teacher, I focus my expectations on the process, not the product. I do not expect finished works of art, but I do expect strong conviction and strong decision-making as the day-by-day process unfolds. To facilitate this, I ask the class to follow these steps: First, color every shape they make on the page; second, use more than one color, at least three; third, cover all the white areas with as little scribbling as possible; fourth, color within the lines (quite difficult for beginners, and I do not stress its importance too much, for it is a skill they must learn by practice); fifth, press down with the crayon hard enough to make clear color strokes (the ones who are more comfortable with a lighter touch are also encouraged, as it is important that each child find his or her own way); and sixth, use colors in a representational way.

For some of my stories I might also urge them to use symbolic colors, such as gold for the story of King Midas whose golden touch turned everything to gold, even his two children. In the story, *Rainbow Rider*, desert brown might be used to show the isolation and the loneliness of the Indian boy who did not have a friend. Flaming orange and yellow might be used to illustrate a sun too hot to be borne in the story, "The Day the Dinosaurs Disappeared from the Earth." Red used for the eyes of the dragon might symbolize evil intent and the hot orange flame from its mouth the destructiveness of fire. Green for a boy's face can symbolize illness—the upset stomach that keeps him from playing soccer. Such symbolic use of color must flow spontaneously from the story. It is not something I consciously try to instill in the curriculum, although it has a powerful effect on the minds of young children when used as part of myth–making in the oral tradition.

Some children reach a point where they want to turn their pictures into art to communicate better than anything yet done. For these high achievers, I suggest further refinements in use of color as a means of raising their minds to a higher pitch and arousing pride in their work. Once they learn to value their own work, they also learn respect for the printed page and recognize how words in books have a high place in their world as communicators of the mind. The step from creating art to creating words is an inevitable and happy process, as natural as a swallow taking flight.

The following are suggestions I offer children ready to take their art to a higher level. I encourage them to place a ground line on their papers delineating spatial zones such as earth and sky. I encourage rudimentary perspective by shaping a house with three sides instead of a frontal view. In the case of mechanical objects such as donut machines and helicopters and jet planes, I suggest showing the four wheels or the x–ray effect of drawings within a drawing. I suggest they place an outline around the picture they have already drawn in pencil, an outline made firmly with black crayon, which enhances and further defines their shapes. This outline has a startling effect, and many of the children are quick to see its advantage in empowering their drawings. With those who like lots of colors and have mastered their fine motor skills by using a rhythmic sweep, I encourage coloring the backgrounds. They do this by moving the side of the crayon back and forth across the page until all the white areas are colored, not just the primary shapes. This is a large step in the life of a child, for they become cognizant that the whole world is a colored place, not just the few objects isolated by drawing. Some of the most imaginative may place colors side–by–side in a checkerboard effect or else create rainbows. The versatility and full vocabulary of these journal students are amazing, and they become a strong models for the other students who may try to branch

44

out and explore more colors. A little healthy copying of such sweeping use of color is good and healthy and should be encouraged. The children who began in September using black or brown or random purple for everything on their pages become transformed by ten months of constant practice into color–perceptive artists—young Monets or Renoirs. Color literacy is the first step to verbal literacy, and these children are well on their way to the mysterious process of reading, the aim of journal class.

In summary, a foundation in drawing and coloring on the preschool level trains the brain in spatial organization and logical procedure. It lays the groundwork for future careers in engineering, math, science, and problem solving. It also stimulates the imagination toward that emotive intensity connected with art, which spurs the activity of reading. "File cabinets" of assimilation, accommodation, and equilibrium are opened up by the proper use of color. Natural beauty in the worlds of young children is enhanced as they begin to notice and perceive in a more complex way. Coloring opens the doors of perception. Most of all, learning to draw and color facilitates the development of decision–making that seeks to isolate and categorize and makes it possible for us to read.

In the next chapter, I show how words, shimmering like so many hundreds of leaves on the tree of knowledge, entice, mystify, and excite the curiosity of young children, inviting them to use their imagination, organize words into sentences, and read.

SARAH
PONY
DRAGON

4. Words! Words! Words!

Now that the children have listened attentively to the story, drawn their pictures, and had their interest heightened by coloring, they are ready to embark on the next step, which is to assign words to their ideas. Words become important because they are powerful symbols that convey meaning. The children are excited because they want to learn to write, that is, to put down their ideas in a symbolic form so that others can receive them.

I explain to them that in ancient days, men made marks with sticks on clay tablets that became "writing." Later, people began to use ink and a sharp pen and drew their mysterious symbols onto animal hides. Still later, paper was invented in China and the invention spread to the West. Monks in their lonely cells spent days and years copying words of sacred scripture until Johann Gutenburg invented the printing press. Suddenly the world was awash with words. In today's world, we cannot avoid words. They are everywhere—on billboards, in books and magazines, on computer screens, or subtitles on movie screens. To the mind of a child, the key that unlocks the mysteries of this world of words is to know how to read and write.

My procedure is to ask the children one at a time to look at their drawings. I say, "What does your drawing tell you? Describe what is happening." From many possibilities, they must choose which word or words they will use. They name or label the theme and thereby strengthen the picture–word association in their own minds. I write the chosen words in upper and lower case on a tent–shaped piece of folded cardboard I place in front of them. They copy it, to the best of their ability, onto the lined part of their paper. They often cherish these words and want to take home the cardboard I have written for them. At home, they share the words with their parents, thus reinforcing the learning process.

Sometimes the children choose associative meanings. For example in the story of the slime monster, several wrote the word "gooey." When I told the story of "The Princess and the Pea" they wrote "hard pea" without my prompting them. In the story of "Doodles the Dinosaur," Doodles came out of the past to visit our preschool and gave all the children a ride on his back around the playground. Several wrote "fun" as the word they associated with this story. Use of associative words illustrates a further step in learning by which the child begins to think of enlarging concepts relating to a central idea. To explain how this works I refer to the learning model of R.C. Atkinson and Richard M. Shiffrin, two child psychologists who updated Jean Piaget's theory of stages by their model of information processing.

Atkinson and Shiffrin's model of how children learn is similar to computer processing; it is made up of a flow chart involving "stimulus input" to a mind that recognizes sights and sounds (in this case, the story) and stores them briefly. Then the sights and sounds are retrieved for use by the short–term memory, which holds onto this information while the mind processes it, adding data by association (such as the word "fun" the children assigned to riding on Doodles the Dinosaur). The information is then moved to long–term memory, where it stays until the mind retrieves it for use. Then it flows to the "response generator," which results in some kind of human action, in this case the action of writing down the word "fun" to show how the story affected the child. This is a fascinating model of learning since it shows how children use information to create new information that they store in their brains for future use. It further shows how the catalyst of journal writing expands their knowledge.

A vivid story encourages children to write words, and sometimes I use the device of verse to give them ideas. Repetition is a useful tool; I often include little poems that children can catch onto quickly and be inspired by. For example, I told the story of Nanook the Eskimo who wants to learn from the animals the secret of how they keep warm. He carves a magic charm out of a whale's tooth and takes it to each animal—a polar bear, seal, and snow goose. He holds up the charm and says:

> "Polar bear, polar bear,
> I mean you no harm
> tell me, tell me,
> how you keep warm!"

They each tell him how they manage to keep warm at the North Pole: the polar bear by his fur, the seal by his blubber, and the snow goose by his two layers of feathers, regular and down. The snow goose gives him a gift by shaking loose his down feathers so Nanook can make a warm jacket, and thus the story has a satisfying ending.

In another story, "The Os Think They Are Perfect," I tell how the letter Os leave the rest of the alphabet because they think they are perfect. They are circles with nothing sticking out or left unattached so they must be perfect! They leave the toy rocking horse, doll and blocks with blanks where the Os should be, and float to the ceiling where they make a circle of mutual admiration around a heart while dancing and chanting:

> "We're so perfect!
> We're so fine!
> We'll be each other's
> Valentine!"

49

The children had a favorable response to this story and many of them chanted what the Os had said while they drew on their papers.

I am less interested in the mechanics of writing than in the meaning the children attach to it. I point out that they should try to write on the line and not make their letters dance above it in a disorganized fashion. I tell them to try to align their letters so they are more or less straight, but I do not like to dwell too much on the perfection of writing their letters because, in this course, it is the power of the words' meaning that I am emphasizing. With practice, the mechanical writing will improve. Some young four–year–olds begin by doing "pre–writing," that is, they cover the page with miscellaneous scribbles they think are words. I steer them to writing just one letter and tell them to do it over and over. Excited shouts signal their triumph: "Hey! I made the letter A!" From that point they can work on other letters. I always insist they write their own names, which brings pride and a sense of self–worth to the project.

Word placement is another issue. When the five–year–olds have perfected their ability to write words that are descriptive or associative with their pictures (usually halfway through the school year in January), I take them to the next level and suggest they try writing sentences. This is much harder for them because they must think in terms of action, using a subject and a predicate. I always ask, "What is happening in your picture? Describe it to me." They tell me with their words and I say "Good! Now write it down." I rephrase the sentence for them, then write it on the tent–folded piece of cardboard for them to copy. "That's a lot of words," they often say. "But you can handle it," I tell them. "Just write what you know." Most of them are able to write the complete sentence and always make a large dot at the end for a period. "Why do we need the dot?" they ask. And I reply, "Because it shows one complete thought. If you want to write another complete thought, you need to separate it by using the period." I encourage them to reach for the stars: "Someday you will be able to write a whole book!" I collect all the papers at the end of the class, and using small print, write their names and the date in the upper left hand corner so that I can file the pages in each child's file folder later on. I write the title of the story at the bottom of the page so they can remember it when they go over it with their parents. When I hand their completed "books" back to them, they always ask in glee, "What story was this?" Their enthusiasm is a splendid moment for me.

Some of the sentences that children have written are listed below, exactly as they wrote them:

"The girl married the frog prince."
"The hot box was in the donut maker."
"The boy aete pancakes."
"The boy opend a chocolate factory."
"I an my boyfriend ate the chocoate factroy."
"The spider is flying."
"The Maple Trees are dripping sap."
"The Os left the rocking horse."
"The dragon turned into a dove of love."

Spacing needs to be worked on in such sentences as:

"Givemy dollback please."
"Thehorse fliedup tothehouse."

Word order needs to be addressed in these sentences:

"The boy to get went Maple syrup."
"Airplane the wheels had Hannah."

Also, they sometimes put their names right in the middle of the sentence with hilarious results: "The snake chased Matthew the cow."

After some good-natured laughter, I point out that their names must be written separately from their sentences. Laughter is the shortest distance between people, and it certainly helps when doing journal writing, provided it doesn't get out of hand.

The ripple effect is also very useful. When a child writes a complete sentence, and I praise him, the others also want to write complete sentences. There is no limit to the enthusiasm of children once an idea excites them.

It is this enthusiasm that inspires them to tackle really difficult, long words such as brontosaurus, Billabong, or Chocolate Factory. They all wanted to write "Rumpelstiltskin" when I told that story. It shows that four and five-year-olds are often at the peak of their mental powers when their enthusiasm is aroused by writing during journal class.

Now to discuss the force of words when used in a journal story. Vibrant use of words is what causes preschool children to want to own words for themselves, to remember them, and to incorporate them into their working vocabulary. Heard as part of an exciting story, these words make an indelible pattern in the thought-processes of young children. Each step of the process—asking for the word, copying it, taking it home to show their parents and having their parents exclaim over their work—causes great excitement for children and makes them want to write and read.

Here are some uses of words that children love. First of all, they enjoy word play. Once, when the letter for the week was N, I told a story about a boy, Ned, who went to stay with his grandfather while his parents were away on a trip. The grandpa could not hear very well. "I'm hungry!" said Ned. "I want some noodles." The grandpa scribbled on a piece of paper and handed it to Ned. "Here, Ned, here are your doodles!" (laughter) "No, Grandpa, I want some noodles!" and Grandpa said, "Okay, Ned, let's go to the pet store and I'll buy you some poodles!" (more laughter) "No, No, Grandpa," said Ned, shouting, "I said *noodles!*" So Grandpa opened up a package of Sarah Lee and handed it to Ned, "Here are your streudels!" (they're rolling in the aisles) "Maybe we'd better go to the ear doctor and get you a hearing aid, Grandpa," said Ned. (I explain what this is) They went to the ear doctor and Grandpa got a hearing aid, then he heard what Ned was saying. "Okay, we'll go to the store," said Grandpa, and he bought Ned four kinds of noodles, linguini, rigatoni, shells, and spaghettios. Ned tried them all, but he liked the spaghettios the best.

I asked the class to draw and write their favorite noodles. One boy drew a house; inside was a table with trays of noodles, all duly labeled. This imaginative word play spurred them to write words.

Another useful tool is assonance, but don't overdo it or it will get stale. The writings of Dr. Seuss are of much help here. When I told the story about "Silly Sammy Slick who drank six sodas and got sick! sick! sick," the children wanted to know what was wrong with him. I said he had gas. This caused much hilarity, and one of the boys drew "Gas-X" on his paper and asked for that word. Empowerment!

Children love words of causality, the logical progression from one idea to the next. In the story about Harry the Horse I told of a horse who is bothered by flies biting his ears. He stops suddenly and refuses to pull the cart full of bricks. (why bricks?) Because Harry's dad is building a wall. (why?) To keep the coyotes out of his yard. Harry lives in Pelham, New Hampshire, and the children are excited by this fact because that is where most of them live. There are real coyotes. Mom gives the boy, Jimmy, who is hero of this story, a magnifying glass (why?) So he can look at Harry the Horse's ears. He does so and sees a giant fly. (I draw a fly magnified on the chalkboard) Jimmy gets his dad's hat and puts it over the horse's ears, thus keeping the flies away. The horse can once again pull the cart loaded with bricks to make the wall to keep the coyotes out of the yard. The children were interested in these words of causality, especially the coyote who, as the danger element in the story, stood out in their minds.

Children are often surprised by the unexpected word that jumps at them out of the context of the story. One journal story was about Little Itch, the seven–year–old witch, who was too young to ride a broomstick on Halloween. She pleaded with the big witches that she be allowed to give out the treats to the trick–or–treaters who would come to the door. She put a jack–o'–lantern in the window so the children would know that hers was a good house to come to, but she didn't know what would be a good treat. The grown–up witches gave her a cookbook of food for children. So when the first trick–or–treaters came to the door, she gave them a pickle! (laughter) No, that wasn't right. She tried again. Next time she gave a hot dog, which was still not right. So next time she gave a bowl of spaghetti. "Eeeeuuu!" said the trick–or–treaters and ran away. Little Itch was sad. She was getting it all wrong. So she went to her Uncle Magic, and he suggested she try something sweet. She went to her potion book and caldron and brewed the most wonderful treat, a gollypop! When the children who came to her door got the gollypops they licked them, and cried "Oh Golly! This is good!" They were so happy they went floating up to the clouds. They stayed up there until the gollypops were all gone, and then they gently floated back to earth again. Little Itch's treat had been a success.

The children were so stimulated by this story, which fell a few days before Halloween, they all asked for the word "gollypop," and some asked for "pickle," "hot dog" and "spaghetti" as well. The out–of–context word is as surprising as a jack–in–the–box and can bring forth joyful sensations, causing children to want to remember and write.

Metaphor is also a powerful tool. The metaphors for preschool children must be, of necessity, simple and easy to grasp, which is why I used color or descriptive metaphor in the story of the three little cats. This is the story of three little cats, a pure white one called "Whitey," a black and gray striped one called "Stripey," and an orange and brown calico cat called "Patchy." The image of the cats came first, the metaphor of how they looked came second, and the combination stayed in the children's minds. The cats wanted to be a part of the Halloween fun. "We must turn black," said Whitey, "so we can walk across the path of the children and bring them bad luck. Everyone knows that if a black cat crosses your path on Halloween, you will have bad luck." The other two cats objected. "But that would be a bad thing to do!" said Stripey. "I want to bring them good luck." Patchy spoke up. "I know what we can do. Let's go see Little Itch the witch and ask her to turn us black just for the night, but to make it so good luck comes to the children." They went to see Little Itch. She whipped up a potion out of bat's wings, black ashes, and licorice sticks, all black things, and she told them to drink it. Whitey, Stripey and Patchy all turned black. They went out on Halloween and yowled, "Good luck! Good luck! We bring you good luck!" to the children, and they did. There never was a happier Halloween with more candy, more sharing and more fun. The next day, the three black cats turned back into Whitey, Stripey and Patchy once again.

These images of three different colored cats were prominent in the minds of the children when they drew their pictures, and they took great pains to depict them exactly as described through use of the metaphor. The three names, Whitey, Stripey, and Patchy, were much asked for as they wrote them on their papers.

Another good device to use that implants words firmly is onomatopoeia sounds, including explosive sounds that arise like volcanic eruptions in the heart of the story. For journaling, I told the story of the mouse family who took up its winter home inside our snow blower. This was not very smart of the mice. My son got out the snowblower to test it before the big snows came. He started the engine and it went "putta putta putt *voom!*" Clouds of black smoke came out. *"Voom! Boom!"* went the snowblower. The entire family of mice leaped out and scattered in all directions, squeaking "Help! Help!" My son pulled out the wads of cotton and fiber that they had used to make their nest in the very engine of the snowblower. What happened to the mice? They went to live with their cousin, Gus, who had made his winter home in a snug tunnel underground.

The children wrote the words "snowblower," "Boom!" "Voom!" and "fiber," which was a new word that they wanted to know what it meant. Such use of new words also stirs up the imagination. The power of onomatopoeia cannot be underestimated, but once again, it must be used sparingly. If serving up words to these children each day is like preparing a nutritious dinner, then onomatopoeia is the very rich and satisfying chocolate sweet to be eaten with moderation.

Words that come in pairs, opposites that "talk to each other," are useful in stimulating the minds of preschoolers. They also teach contrast, an important discipline involved in problem-solving. One day I told the story about zero based on the letter of the week which was Z. The balanced opposites were "hot" and "cold," and "above" and "below."

Two Eskimo children, Chinook and Nanook, a boy and a girl, lived near the North Pole where it was very cold. One day they went for a walk and tried to find the North Pole. They found it, a red and white striped pole with the word "North" written on the top. Right next to the North Pole was a giant thermometer with liquid mercury in it and marks on the side. The word "zero" was beside the biggest mark in the middle. (A drawing on chalkboard showed a giant thermometer.) All the marks below zero were blue to show coldness and all the marks above zero were red to show heat. The children read the temperature, which was way below zero. They wanted to find out what would happen if the temperature went up above zero. So they built a fire and warmed up the thermometer until the mercury rose and rose. It went way up above 32 degrees. Everything started melting. The polar bear came to them and complained he could not catch any seals for his dinner because the ice was melting and they all stayed in the water. The whales complained that the water was too *hot*. The seagulls complained that there were no icebergs left for them to land on—it was getting too *hot* and they were all melting. All the animals pleaded with the children to put out the fire. So they did. The temperature in the giant thermometer fell back to below zero and everything got *cold*. The animals at the North Pole were happy once again.

Most of the children drew the North Pole and huge thermometers. They wrote "above zero," "below zero," "hot," "cold," "seal," and "polar bear" on their papers.

Such are some of the devices used in my journal class to elicit an enthusiastic response from preschool children. They looked forward to coming to class and threw themselves into their work, opening up their minds to receive the words I served to them in forms of wordplay, assonance, causality, the use of unexpected words, metaphor, onomatopoeia, and paired opposites.

Isak Dinesen, author of *Out Of Africa* and the short stories *Winter's Tales*, described the power of words most succinctly in *Of Hidden Thoughts and of Heaven*: "I was thinking of those small instruments that we call words, and by which we have to manage in this life of ours. I was thinking of how, by interchanging two everyday words in an everyday sentence, we alter our world. For when you had spoken, I first thought 'Is that possible?'—then secondly, after a moment, 'That is possible.'"

It is possible to teach children the meaning of words in journal class by picture-word association, by description, by repetition, and by information processing. Use of rhymes in the story helps to cement words firmly because children are responsive to the imaginative nuances of the human voice. Whole sentences can be taught once children have mastered the basics of writing down what their pictures mean. The mechanics of writing is less important than the process, and the children themselves discover rich rewards as they read over what they have written to go with their drawings and colorings. The first three steps of the process—listening to the story, drawing the picture, and coloring the picture—have led up to the supreme act of putting words with the picture. The children learn that words are powerful tools that enable them to read. Now I will turn to the dynamic foundation of word use—the story.

5. Story as Dynamic Foundation

Hearing a story aloud is different from silently reading information in a book. Storytelling arises from our nurturing and knowledge–acquiring instincts and is a form of loving exchange between the teller and the listener. It was the vehicle that prehistoric men and women used to pass down their tribal culture and survival skills to their young. The tribal storyteller occupied a position of power, often as a shaman or priest, and used stories in various forms such as chants to guide the people. Thus, the telling of stories was important not only to educate the young but also to maintain order and to preserve the intellectual and cultural content of the society as a whole. Storytelling provided a dynamic foundation for the civilizations of Hebrews, Sumerians, Greeks, Norsemen, and the peoples of India and Persia. In North America it remains an important element among many native peoples who include storytelling, singing, and chanting in their religious rituals.

These are historic examples of storytelling, but all oral traditions have certain things in common. Whether it's a tale spun by an elder beside the tribal fire or one designed by a pre-school teacher to inspire little children to want to read, a story related vocally arouses curiosity, stimulates imagination, awakens memory and strengthens it. Amazement, humor, wit, and excitement leap like electricity from the teller to the listeners. It has been proven that people remember ideas and events from a story far longer than they will from reading straight facts.

Learning to retain knowledge is one of the vital educational tools pre-readers can acquire through the storytelling process. Children learn to listen to sequences of cause and effect, to identify with heroes who may give validity to people and things they enthusiastically believe in, and to follow adventures that are satisfying because they are a part of their world. Memory skills are heightened as they follow the action and repetition of a well thought-out story. Skills to be developed in first grade are memorizing phonics, phonemes, vowel and consonant sounds, words in sequence, sentences, and eventually the smooth and efficient reading of entire paragraphs.

Learning to read is a step-by-step process and listening to stories attentively is where it begins. Children in my journal class are alerted that the story is in the words that are in the books, and that learning to listen well is crucial to unlock the meaning of the printed word.

Prereading and prewriting skills are all too often overlooked, but their omission may result in a child's having difficulty in learning to read in first grade. A year or more of journal writing class lays a foundation for the intense mental activity that is involved in learning to read. Remember, it is the execution of the process itself that provides this preparation, and it is the preschool teacher's job to stimulate the child to action by telling the best stories in the most exciting way. The following are storytelling tips.

Command the children's attention. Be a performer and show off! It has been said that teaching is one-fourth preparation and three-fourths dramatic presentation. When journal class begins, the children should be sitting in their chairs with no toys on the table. They should be attentive and ready to listen. Such sayings as "One, two, three, all eyes on me" help to focus their minds on the teacher. You can begin with, "For your story today. . . " or the old standby "Once upon a time. . . " Project your voice as an actor does and vary the tone using loud and soft effects. Make judicious use of pauses to emphasize dramatic sections.

Use your sense of humor. A little laughter shows your audience is paying attention and spreads vitality through the group.

Involve the children in the story. Pause to ask open-ended questions that relate to the subject. Also ask questions of those children who are not paying attention because this brings them back on track.

Tell stories that children can identify with, making them relative by including characters of their same age, or ones who live in the same town. Children always recognize their addresses and get excited when the story happens close to home. Use the important events of their lives, like birthdays or holidays. Birthday parties are especially effective because these are milestones to young children. So much growing is done and so much of the world is conquered between the birthdays of two to six years. Adults can scarcely imagine the extraordinary increase in knowledge of the world that a child experiences during these years. Effective storytelling can contribute to this growth process.

Tell stories that are upbeat, positive, exciting and encouraging. Avoid topics of despair, horror, or death. Satire is not appropriate because little children cannot understand it. This is not the time for them to doubt or mock the world; they are too busy immersing themselves in the abundance of life. Children have often acted out on the playground a story they have heard in journal class, so deeply does it affect them. So it is important to serve the healthiest and most delightful stories possible. This does not mean that stories cannot have themes of evil versus good or speak of conflicts at the heart of the human condition, but they must be cast into a form appropriate for children.

Listening skills are an active and important part of the teaching–learning process. The teacher must listen to children to gain feedback and to know how their stories are being received, and the children must learn to listen attentively to the teacher. Listening is the process used to convert spoken language into meaning in the mind. It is neither automatic nor passive, but is a skill that must be learned. It is a sad statistic but a true one that adults seldom listen with more than 25 percent of their full attention, and yet they expect children to listen with 100 percent capacity. If children talk too much during the story or look bored or gaze out the window, then whose fault is it? Yours! Retrieve the children's attention by taking the story through an abrupt turn of events, or by inserting onomatopoeia, or a surprising word. Having undivided attention is not an impossible achievement, and it is especially gratifying to see the children sitting utterly and completely quiet, their eyes fixed on your face, as they take in your story. As the year progresses, such attention will happen more and more frequently as you polish your dramatic storytelling skills. I know children are responding to my story when they fling themselves into the drawing and coloring activity and talk excitedly about the words they will use. This is the surest indicator of how well they have been listening.

Use a visual aid while presenting stories to capture attention by drawing simple but lively pictures on the chalkboard. You don't have to be an artist to draw simple shapes such as a circle, triangle, square, or rectangle. People, faces, and animals can all be reduced to these elementary shapes. Such illustrations are like magic to children, and as the story unfolds, you may add details to them as you talk. Chalkboard drawing is preferable to prepared pictures because it is a dynamic activity that the children can watch as you talk. As you model how to draw, this empowers the children as well.

The use of props also enhances the telling of a story. One day I brought two summer squash, two green tomatoes, and one red tomato to journal class. I passed the vegetables around so that all the children could touch, feel and look at them. Then I told the following story about Tom and his sister Tara (the letter of the week was "T"):

Tom and Tara grew prize vegetables that they wished to take to the fair. (I described planting, watering and weeding and told how sunlight helped the vegetables grow) As summer went on, Tara saw big yellow squash flowers but no squash. Tom saw lots of tomatoes, but they were all green. Would they have any vegetables to take to the fair? They asked their Grandfather Old Travis. "Just wait!" said the wise old grandfather. "All things ripen with time." (concept of the passage of time) Two more weeks passed and suddenly butternut squash covered the ground. Soon they were ripe and ready to go to the fair, and Tom's big plump tomatoes turned red. Tara and Tom won blue ribbons for the best vegetables in the state and were very happy.

As for telling the story, follow this formula. First, provide an introduction presenting the characters and their ages and make a few brief remarks to establish the setting. Begin the action right away, for preschoolers are impatient with exposition and long descriptions. Have the good guys and the bad guys clearly delineated and state the objectives of each if that is the type of story you are telling. Have the action rise sequentially, and use repetition to build tension until you reach the climax. Follow Edgar Allen Poe's diagram of how a short story should be written: Begin quickly; develop the action; hit the peak; and have a quick denouement.

As Isak Dinesen said, "Be loyal to the story . . . . Hear then, where the storyteller is loyal to the story, there, in the end, silence will speak. Where the story has been betrayed, silence is but emptiness. But we, the faithful, when we have spoken our last word, will hear the voice of silence." When the story is told from the heart, with logical building of idea upon idea, the ending will allow the listener to think within the silence that follows it. It is within these silences that profound enjoyment, ideas, images, and new values will surface. Then the story has been successful.

Journal class stories should be told in five minutes, or at

the most, ten. To achieve concision and clarity, the story must be very well rehearsed. I allow five to ten minutes of class time for the story, and fifteen minutes for drawing and coloring. The last ten or fifteen minutes is for writing. This gives the children sufficient time to complete their work, provided they are attentive and adhere to my standards. It is important for them to complete all four steps of the journal writing process, for that is what will eventually lead to their learning to read.

At the beginning of the year when the class is still learning the process, the stories are very simple. As the year goes on, I increase the intricacy as the children scaffold their experiences, train their memories, and increase their mental endurance.

You can obtain stories from books, magazines, radio and television. Even the encyclopedia is a good resource. All offer interesting plots that can be reduced to a child's level through controlled use of vocabulary, but remember that too rudimentary a story is insulting to their intellects, and they will quickly get bored with it. Fairy tales are a source, but many of these are full of violence; they need to be carefully screened and altered in places to be made acceptable to little children. We need to sift out anything that causes children to be genuinely fearful or teach them bad habits. Once the teacher has learned the knack of storytelling, has discovered the elements that please, delight and amaze, and deleted those to be left out, then the teacher is ready to create stories.

It is common to tell stories to preschoolers by introducing a "letter of the week," which the children learn by craft project or writing using sand, paint, or pencil. Fine motor control and memory skills are developed as each child learns to make these mysterious marks which, when strung together, form words. If the letter of the week is "N," each day I tell a story that contains a large number of "Ns," especially in those words associated with the main theme. As the children are seating themselves at the table, I ask them to count the number of "Ns" on the chalkboard, where I have labeled each of my drawings with the word that best describes it. The children get experience all week in writing the letter "N" in both upper and lower case, which they remember from the stories.

For example, on Monday of "N" week, I retold Rudyard Kipling's "Just So Story" of how Elephant Child got his long nose. On Tuesday I told a story called "The Turtle Doesn't Like His Neck." The turtle is envious of the necks of an owl, a giraffe, and a monkey, and wishes he could be like them, until they each explain the disadvantages of their necks and the advantage of his—he can hide his head within his shell and be safe from danger. On Wednesday, I told the story of Nancy who tries on her mom's necklace made of pearls and then goes to bake a cake. The necklace breaks and the pearls fall into the cake batter. "Oh no!" says Nancy, "How will I get it out?" Her big sister Nellie says, "Don't bother trying to take out the pearls. Bake them in the cake. It will be a surprise cake!" So Nancy bakes the cake and when her mom bites into the cake, surprise! She finds her necklace.

On Thursday, I retold the Beatrix Potter story, *The Tale Of Timmy Tiptoes*, with a rhyme sung by the birds—"Who's been diggin' up my nuts?" And on Friday I told the story about Sinbad the Sailor who was shipwrecked on an island of dinosaurs and found a giant nest, as big as a swimming pool. He climbed inside it to escape from a T-Rex and an enormous bird called a Roc landed on him. Sinbad tied himself to its leg using his belt, and when it flew up into the sky, he went with it. They flew to a faraway city called Numinor where he cut himself loose and lived to tell many a tale of his adventures.

The following is a story that I made up, in which I point out the useful tools of dialogue, repetition, rising action, sequence building, suspense mounting to a climax, and finally, an upbeat ending. I show how these elements converge to make an enjoyable experience for the children and an impetus to successful journal writing.

The story originated with a baby snapping turtle only about two days old that my husband had found in a sand pit near his office and brought home for the children to see. I took it to school in a white bowl with a rock in the middle, which was surrounded with about three inches of water. I placed the bowl on the table and invited the preschoolers to have a good look, but warned them not to touch the snapping turtle because its jaw was already developed and it could bite them. This information awed them. I then removed the snapper to a safe place and had them sit at the journal tables. I told this story:

Little Snapper

(Quick introduction, sets place and main theme) Once, by the side of a pond, there was an egg. It was round and white and smooth, but none of the animals that lived near the pond knew what it was. (mystery gets them wondering) The fish swam by it, but they did not know what it was. The birds landed by it, but they did not know what it was. The frogs swam and hopped around it, but it was too big and hard to be frog's eggs, so they didn't know either. (note repetition, a memory device)

One day the egg cracked (sudden action) and out came an amazing creature. (arouses curiosity) He had a knobby head with a sharp beak, a long skinny neck, a tail, and four scratchy legs. (description challenges the children to picture an image) But the most interesting thing about him was that he carried his house on his back in the shape of a huge, bony shell.

Can you guess it? "It's a turtle!" say the children. (feeling of reward for putting a concept with the description) "Snap! Snap!" went his mouth and he grabbed a fish and ate it. "I am a snapping turtle!" (enlarge on the concept of what a snapping turtle is by what it does) In one week, he ate almost all the fish that lived in the pond. He also ate the dragonflies that landed on the pond. He was always hungry.

(Action, introduce a new character) One day a boy came

by and saw the turtle as he lay like a log in the shallow water. Quietly the boy sneaked up behind him and picked him up. "Oh Boy! A turtle! I caught him and I am going to take him home and keep him forever!" (how did the turtle feel—shift point of view) Little Snapper twisted his head this way and that and moved all his legs as if he was running, but he could not get away. The boy carried him home and put him in a white bowl that his mom gave him. They added a rock and some water. Little Snapper was very sad. He missed his pond, his fish, and his friends the frogs. He cried big turtle tears, but no one noticed.

(Now the climax) The boy took Little Snapper to school to show all his friends. "Oh no!" said his teacher (opposition through dialogue). "That is a snapping turtle! He can live to be a hundred years old, and when he gets big, his jaws can snap a broom handle in two, or even a boy's wrist. (element of danger) You better let him go back to the mud of the pond." So the boy thought about it, and then let him go. Little Snapper was very happy to be in his familiar pond once again (upbeat ending).

"And that's your story for today!" Only when this cue is given do you pass out the pencils and the paper. If the materials are on the table during the storytelling, the children tend to fold, roll, crumple the papers, spin their pencils, compare them to their neighbors, and be distracted from the story.

"Now you can begin your drawing." Give them time to think. If your story produced the "silence that speaks," then they will really concentrate and the room will fall quiet as they search for a theme to draw. This is a rewarding time when pencils in the hands of young artists produce amazing results.

In the next chapter I discuss types of stories. As there are quite a number of them, each will be examined in turn for the advantage it offers to the teacher who must think up something new and exciting to tell each day.

6. An Assembly of Ideas: Story Types

There are many types of stories that the inventive teacher draws upon in her daily search for new ideas. The journal teacher wants stories that generate excitement, but this results only if the teacher is excited and takes the story to heart by rehearsing it ahead of time, usually at home where there is no pressure to perform. I find it helpful to write down the story. Thorough preparation helps the teller be relaxed, confident, and alert enough to make the changes that become necessary in response to cues from the children during the actual performance.

Stories of suspense are always exciting, and ask mysterious questions for children to unravel while the plot increases in degrees of complexity. One example is Hans Christian Andersen's *The Tinder Box*, where we begin by meeting a penniless soldier. An old lady, who is actually a witch, asks him if he would like to make his fortune. How? She tells him to move a rock and go underground through a tunnel until he gets to a cave. There he will meet a guard dog with eyes as large as saucers who is guarding a treasure. He is not to take the treasure but to go on until he meets a dog with eyes as big as soup plates who is guarding another treasure. Then, he is to go on past that dog (suspense is building) and find a dog with eyes bigger still, eyes as big as truck wheels, who is guarding a little tinder box. The soldier may fill his pockets with treasure, but he must bring the tinder box to the witch. So he goes down into the tunnel and (repeat each meeting with the dogs in a gradually amplified voice) he does all that she tells him, but he decides to keep the tinder box. His justification for this is that she is a witch and means to do no good. A little later he goes into town, where he is arrested for looking at the princess and wanting to marry her. He is thrown in jail and is utterly sad and miserable, until he remembers he can still smoke his pipe because he has the tinder box. He strikes it and the first dog appears to him. "This is a mighty wonder!" he says and strikes it again and the second dog appears. He strikes the box the third time and the mightiest dog of all appears. With these strong dogs he escapes from prison, humbles the king, and gains the daughter's hand in marriage.

This is an example of a mystery story with lots of suspense and a happy ending for the poor soldier. The children loved it, especially the description of the dogs' eyes being as large as saucers, soup plates, or truck wheels. They liked how this increase in size bore a magical relation to the dogs' supernatural strength.

Another popular story type depicts a journey in which the characters must obtain something of value. They encounter many difficulties in sequences that rise to a climax of danger. A resolution is achieved when the danger is vanquished and the ending is peaceful. Such a story is "The Waters of Life," about a little girl who went to see her grandmother, a wrinkled old figure (drawn on the chalkboard) who said, "I am dying, dearest granddaughter. I want you to have my blue pearl necklace." The girl weeps and says, "Oh Grandma, I won't let you die," but she takes the necklace. "Only the waters of life can save me now," says the grandmother. The little girl sets out through the forest to find it. After a time, she meets a griffin, a terrible winged creature with the head of an eagle and the body of a lion. "Give me your necklace," says the griffin, "and I will show you the waters of life." At first the girl says "No!" but then she overcomes her fear and flings the necklace around its shaggy neck. It roars and arches its back and leaps in the air. Suddenly, great white wings sprout from its shoulders and it stands before her, a beautiful white winged horse. "Climb on my back and we'll fly to the waters of life," says the horse, so the little girl climbs onto its back. With a surge of power, they rise from the ground and fly above the clouds for many miles. Below them, the earth is green until they come to a tall mountain, where the waters of life lie in a jewel blue lake. The little girl finds a pitcher beside a stone, scoops up water from the lake, then mounts the winged horse and they fly back to her grandmother. The horse waits outside while she goes in and gives Grandma a drink. Instantly, the lines are smoothed away from the old lady's face (erase the lines from the grandmother's face drawn on the chalkboard) and she says, "My, I feel like dancing and singing and baking chocolate chip cookies with you." She was young again!

Perhaps the simplest type of story to tell is the expository, or "show and tell" story that uses distinct items, related either by cause or comparison, in ways that highlight them as themes. For example, an expository story about garden vegetables shows that Jim and his sister Jill each decided to grow a vegetable garden. Jim said he would grow vegetables that grew with the part that we eat under the ground. He grew radishes, carrots, turnips, potatoes and onions. Jill grew vegetables that develop above the ground: beans, peas, lettuce, squash, and tomatoes. I drew each vegetable clearly on the chalkboard, showing it to be above or below the ground. This taught the concepts of "above" and "below" as well as the several types of vegetables.

Another expository story is "The Bug Show." Nancy and Bob, brother and sister, decided to go into the woods and fields with their collecting boxes and bring their insects home for a bug show, which Grandpa would judge. Nancy caught a grasshopper, a butterfly, and a ladybug. Bob caught a tomato worm, a stag beetle, and an ant. (draw pictures on chalkboard) Grandpa said the butterfly was beautiful, the grasshopper could sing all day and make people happy, and the ladybug had a sense of duty because she was hurrying home to save her family from a fire. All of Nancy's insects were good ones! About Bob's insects Grandpa said the tomato worm with its large green body and red spots was the most striking to look at, as well as being the hungriest (he could eat his way through a whole tomato in less than an hour). The stag beetle with his sharp horns was the most scary, and the ant, for all its small size, could lift huge pebbles that were seven times its own weight. "The ant wins," said Grandpa, "because any bug that can lift seven times its own weight is like a super-bug." Children were affected by the novelty of the idea that bugs can do different things and that the most spectacular looking ones aren't necessarily the best. For the children who loved nature this was a fun story, and for the rest it was intriguing and awakened new awareness. The aim of a good story is to expand consciousness, and "The Bug Show" certainly did this.

The stories that tell "how to do it" are always of great interest to children, particularly if the subject comes from their own experience. For example, I retold the story of "Cindy Bakes A Funny Cake" from a Hallmark Original Pop-up Book (1962). The book described how to make a cake the right way, by using butter and sugar, eggs, flour and milk, and mixing them together to form a batter that is cooked in the oven. Many children in journal class had done this since we bake at preschool frequently. In the story Cindy was only six, and she wasn't sure how to bake a birthday cake for her mother. She mixed in butter and eggs and flour and sugar. Then she mixed in ketchup and mustard ("Eeeeeuuui!" said all the children), and worst of all, she added yeast! "Yeast rises and rises and is what makes air bubbles in bread," I told them. Was that a good idea? To put yeast into a cake?" "No-o-o!" said the children. Pleased with herself, Cindy put the cake in the oven and turned it on to 350 degrees. The cake began to rise and rise within the oven. Suddenly it was too big for the oven to hold and began pouring out through the oven door. It filled up the whole kitchen with red gooey mess. (red because of the ketchup) Cindy struggled across the cakey-kitchen and called her big sister who was upstairs. Sister came down and turned off the oven. She helped Cindy clean up the mess left by the yeasty cake. Then the two of them together made a cake the right way for their mother's birthday. This story, in addition to being a "how to do it" story, caused a great deal of healthy laughter at the foibles of Cindy and her yeasty cake. A sense of humor contributes to positive exuberance that helps journal writers do their best work.

Stories about science and math are also very popular. The story about Gauss' Law, which to jaded adults may sound tiresome, is fresh and exciting for children. Karl Gauss lived from 1777 to 1855. He worked with electromagnetic units of magnetic flux density and proved that electricity travels around an enclosed metal object, not through it. To demonstrate, I told the story of James and Harriet, a brother and sister both six-years-old, who went on a picnic to the country with Mom and Dad. They were very happy as they spread out the pie, the sandwiches, and the chocolate cake under a large tree. Suddenly a dark cloud came up and it began to rain. "Was it a good idea for them to stay under the tree?" I asked the children. "It may stay dry under there." This set them to thinking. Some said "Yes," and some said "No." I said, "No, it was a bad idea." Suddenly lightning began to fork down from the clouds in great zig zags and strike the ground. The smell of lightning was everywhere, and the bright light blinded their eyes. "Back to the car!" shouted Mom and Dad. "Run!" The entire family got up and ran. On the way, they had to run through a stream. "Was it a good idea for them to have their feet wet in the stream with lightning all around?" I asked the children. "No!" they said but did not know why. "No," I echoed, "because lightning strikes people who are standing in water." They got into their car and shut the door. Now they were safe. "Why were they safe?" I asked. Some children said because the tires were made of rubber, which does not conduct electricity. "That's a good answer but not the right one," I said. "They were safe because of Gauss' Law." I drew lightning striking against the car with arrows going all around it in two directions. "Gauss' Law states that if lightning strikes an enclosed metal object, such as a car, the lightning charge will go around its outside and not go into it or through it." The children drew pictures of cars on their papers with lightning striking and little arrows going around the outside of the cars. They wrote "Gauss' Law," "Lightning," and "Rainstorm." They were carried away by this story, which taught them a true scientific fact.

Another science story is "Uncle Bernard Discovers Iodine." Bernard Courtois discovered iodine in 1812 when he found violet crystals of the substance in burnt seaweed. In his lab he performed experiments that turned the crystals into liquid and discovered iodine's properties as a medicinal disinfectant. My lively story told how he and his fictional nephew went for a walk on the beach, discovered violet crystals in burnt seaweed, and then worked together in the lab to make liquid iodine. The nephew cut his leg with an axe, and Uncle Bernard poured the iodine on the cut to stop it from getting infected. The children could relate to this story because we apply a topical solution to their cuts when they scrape their knees in the playground.

"Jimmy and the Inchworm" is a math story. Jimmy's preschool teacher hands out rulers and explains that each ruler is marked by 12-inch lengths. For homework, each one in the class had to bring in something as long as 12 inches in a ruler. They were allowed to take their rulers home to measure things. Jimmy sat down under a tree and did not know what to do. Every stick he found on the ground was either too long or too short, and when he tried to break them, they never came out right. As he lay there, a little green worm lowered itself down on a silken thread right before his face. "Who are you?" he asked. "I am an inchworm. I am exactly one inch long." "Show me!" cried Jimmy and put up his ruler. The inchworm showed Jimmy he was exactly one inch long by lying down on the ruler. "If only there were 12 of you," said Jimmy. "But there are!" said the worm. He called up into the tree, "Come down! Come down!" and a whole lot of little inchworms came down. They laid themselves down on the ruler and were exactly one foot long. "Hooray!" said Jimmy. "Come with me to school." He took the worms to school and they lay down on the ruler in front of the teacher. They enjoyed performing so much that they asked Jimmy to take them to a circus where they did an inchworm act. At the end of the performance they would lie down on a 12-inch ruler. I used rulers as props for this story and the children loved it.

Folk tales or fairy tales can be used with good effect, especially if they are treasured from the teacher's own childhood. Unfortunately, many of these tales are violent with tricky or deceitful characters who suffer horrible endings, since fairy tales were once used by nurses world-wide to chastise little children and scare them into obedience. So it is best to choose fairy tales carefully and change elements that are undesirably violent. For instance, at the end of Jack and the Beanstalk, the giant is climbing down the beanstalk chasing after Jack, whom he intends to kill for taking his golden harp and hen that laid the golden eggs. But Jack reaches the ground first, gets an axe and cuts down the beanstalk while the giant is still making his way down. Instead of having the giant fall to his death and be mashed into a bloody pulp, say: "Do you know what happened to the giant? He fell from a great height to the land in Jack's country and was turned by magical means into a mountain, the Mountain of the Sleeping Giant. If you visit the land where Jack lived you can see the Mountain of the Sleeping Giant there to this day." This gives a sense of closure and a smack of realism by suggesting the children could really visit Jack's country.

Similarly, in the African folk tale, "Akimba and the Magic Cow," Akimba's deceitful, thieving neighbor robbed him of his magic cow and magic hen. The animals were magic because if you said "Kla Kla Kla" or "Bu Ru Ru," they would produce gold or eggs. Next, the neighbor tried to steal a magic stick. He said words of incantation over the stick, expecting a reward, but it flew into the air and began to beat him unmercifully until he begged Akimba to make it stop. Instead of having the stick actually beat this deceitful neighbor, I turned it into a stick that danced with him and would not allow him to stop—not until he had given back to Akimba his magic cow and magic hen. It was more wholesome to have the stick dance than to beat the neighbor, and the moral remained the same: he should not steal.

Stories from history are always welcome, especially if they coincide with a feast such as Thanksgiving. I told the story of the Mayflower and the Speedwell departing from England. The families of pilgrims who journeyed on ships wanted to worship God the way they chose and not the way insisted by the King. By drawing a geographical map line from shore to shore on the chalkboard, I showed how the Speedwell had to turn back because it was leaking, but the Mayflower crossed the Atlantic Ocean. I told how the pilgrims landed near Cape Cod at Plymouth Rock just in time for winter, and cold was the winter so that many died. But in the spring they planted their gardens. It was hard work. I told of Squanto, the Native American, who came out of the great forest and showed them how to bury dead fish near the corn plants to help them grow better. He also taught the pilgrims how to hunt and fish. Then I described the first Thanksgiving when the pilgrims gave a big party after the harvest and invited all the Indians. "There was food for all, pies and turkeys and popcorn," I told them. "This was the first Thanksgiving. We celebrate it in our homes at this time every year. Now you can go home and tell your parents all about it."

Thematic stories based on holidays are very effective in getting children excited about journal writing. You can especially have fun with Halloween. Most preschools highlight this season with a Halloween party where everyone comes in costume, affording the journal teacher a motherlode of storytelling opportunities. A week or so before the actual holiday, you can tell a new "fright story" each day. Easter can be treated with gaily colored pictures of springtime flowers and Easter bunnies dyeing eggs and distributing candy. There is no end to Christmas stories that can be told, but try to emphasize the sharing associated with Christmas and de-emphasize the greediness for gifts.

It is okay to dip into the rich lore of your own past and retell stories by great authors you read and enjoyed as a child. Many stories from *Just So Stories* and *The Jungle Book* by Rudyard Kipling and those from *Winnie The Pooh* by A.A. Milne can be shortened and retold within a five minute oral presentation. I've also used tales from C.S. Lewis' *The Chronicles of Narnia*, from Beatrix Potter, and from two wonderful authors of the 1950s, Margaret Wise Brown and Barbara Cooney. Oscar Wilde's "The Selfish Giant," Edward Eager's "Half Magic," and Dr. Seuss' delightful "Oobleck" were all reworked to fit my oral storytelling. Jane Yolen's picture book, *Rainbow Rider*, lends itself to easy storytelling and is a much-loved tale that the children ask me to tell over and over again. I have even used Ernest Hemmingway's *The Old Man and the Sea* with success. The trick is to condense these sources into a five-minute time period, without losing the essence of the story. Ten or fifteen minutes at most is all that is needed to tell more intricate stories presented in the second half of the year.

Last but not least is mythology. The great tales that have been spun through the ages to explain the concepts closest to the human heart can be a powerful force in teaching little children to read. Like the fairy tales and folk legends, there is a dark side to many myths that may need to be omitted. It would never do to tell how Hercules went mad and slew his wife and children, for example. The judicious rephrasing of the myths can be very inspirational. I always tell the story of King Midas who was given the gift of having everything he touched turn to gold. The king thought this was wonderful until he found he could neither eat nor drink. The touch of his lips turned even food and water to gold and, despite his riches, he was doomed to die of starvation and thirst. I dramatize the pathos of the scene in which his two children ran to him, crying "Daddy! Daddy!" He spread his arms in warning, "No! Don't come near me!" But it was too late. They touched him and turned into gold. It was only by appealing to Bacchus, the god who gave him the cursed gift of the golden touch, that Midas regained his original human state and his children returned to life.

Stories presented early in the year should be simple, direct and easy for the children to follow. As their listening skills improve, children can hear more complex stories. Part two offers the teacher a selection of stories that children like. Since most preschool literature consists of picture books, there is a dearth of existing material well-suited to use in the teaching of journal writing. I have provided stories that are interesting but use limited vocabulary. When read silently, these stories may seem brusque and rudimentary, but this simplicity is deceptive. Children with a very limited attention span (of five to ten minutes) have responded well to this kind of direct, concise format with uncomplicated dialogue. These stories omit many of the details of plot and setting, but such aggrandizements are extraneous and even distracting for young children. Subject matter is limited to those events and experiences that relate to their own lives, which has proven, by classroom experience, to appeal to preschool children.

Read the stories in part two with the intent to teach vigorously. Re-enter the world of childhood, where what seems jaded to adults is still new and fresh to young children. The stories of part two are to be told in succession and gradually incorporated into the curriculum from September to June.

Before I present these stories, however, a chapter on discipline is in order. Positive discipline helps children to focus and keep them on task. Without it, there can be no successful teaching.

7. Discipline: The Cement that Builds

Good discipline is crucial to teaching any level, and at the preschool level, it also requires good humor, positive thinking, and warm feelings for the children. Little children are constantly seeking love, an unconscious desire that exists from birth. They also seek support and approval from adults who offer security and serve as models of behavior. Very young children want to be respected as individuals, but they have not yet developed the habits of ego. In a group situation they look to their peers to define their roles for them. What one or two do, the rest mimic. This is known as the ripple effect because good behavior (or bad) can quickly spread through the group. When all are attentive, focused, comfortable, secure, and happy, all listening to the teacher, this is a "good group." When one or two cause disruptions, whether to get attention, power, or just be silly, they can cause the entire group to go astray and no longer focus on the teacher.

The very challenging task of the preschool teacher is to catch the attention of the group at the outset and hold it until the end, while making the oral presentation of the story as direct and complete as possible. It is important to keep in mind that the attention span of little children is limited. A teacher must be aware that it is not just the individual or "one-on-one" aspect of discipline that needs to be addressed, but also the entire group, which acquires a united personality of its own.

Discipline in the preschool classroom should take place in a climate that is logical, reasonable and responsible. Discipline clears the room of distractions and allows the fresh air of the teacher's thoughts to pour through. It can calm children and encourage their desire to listen; it can keep them "on track" and focused, eager to learn. Discipline is the cement in a pyramid that the teacher and students build together. If the story is the dynamic foundation of this pyramid, then the hard work of the children represents the stones that must be moved and lifted, piece by piece, onto the structure. The children need to feel that learning to journal is a positive experience, and that following the clearly defined rules will enable them to meet the teacher's expectations. This gives them a wonderful sense of security, and if the teacher is able to motivate them with a strong oral presentation of a story, the discipline problems become almost non-existent.

When I began teaching journal class five years ago, I did not have the automatic command of the group that comes with practice. So I applied the principles of two great teachers of discipline in the classroom, Rudolph Dreikurs and Fredric H. Jones. By using their principles, I found that discipline is a creative give-and-take between the students and the teacher, with respect being a large factor on both sides. In a climate of respect, learning blossoms as easily as a rose unfolding in the sun. That upward look of intense interest on the faces of the children was a tremendous encouragement, telling me that I was on the right track. The following are a few of the principles that helped me to build successful classroom discipline.

The Dreikurs Model

Rudoph Dreikurs (1897-1972) was born in Vienna, Austria, and for many years worked with Alfred Adler, a behavioral psychologist. Dreikurs, who came to the United States in 1937, is most important for redefining the idea of discipline, that discipline is not a punishment. Good discipline enables children to take responsibility for their actions, not simply react out of fear of the teacher. The aim of all discipline is self-discipline. The best type of teacher he described is democratic, not autocratic or overly permissive. Dreikurs said that all children want to belong and their misbehavior is due to four mistaken goals that they erroneously think will help them belong. These goals are: (1) attention getting; (2) power seeking; (3) revenge seeking; and (4) displaying inadequacy. According to Dreikurs, to effectively discipline, the teacher must identify which of these four mistaken goals are present in the misbehaving child by using his or her own feelings of being annoyed, threatened, hurt, or powerless. Once having determined which form of behavior the child is acting out, the teacher can take steps to correct it. Dreikurs believes in imposing logical consequences for the misbehavior.

In the case of preschool children, I employ this democratic method by instructing them at the outset what I expect from them in terms of paying attention, following the rules of good journal writing, and getting the work done. If the child does not do these things, he will be warned, once, twice, three times, and he's out. I separate him from the group and make him sit at another table or go to the book corner to join the alternative "non-journal writing" group. This is quite severe, for most children hate to be singled out from the group. After awhile, I will talk with the misbehaving child, and explain that he may rejoin the group if he will "do journal" and stop acting out. In the most severe cases, I tell him I expect better behavior tomorrow, and if he keeps misbehaving, he will not be "invited" to do journal for several days. This reminds the child that doing journal is a privilege, not an automatic right, and as a privilege, it can be taken away.

The Dreikurs method is a respectful and democratic way of handling a class. It works in preschool provided there is a clear statement of the rules at the outset, and "pep talks" throughout the year to keep the children on track. It works slowly, because it depends on the tacit consent and support of the class to succeed. But luckily, the children are willing to learn discipline along with the other lessons of journal class because every day is new and exciting for them, and they are eager to drink up knowledge. They have a mighty thirst!

The Jones Model

Fredric H. Jones is a psychologist and director of the Classroom Management Training Program in Santa Cruz, California. He found that the largest discipline problem was not open defiance of the teacher but time-wasting, usually due to the students talking to one another during the lesson and not paying attention. When it came time for them to do their work, the teacher had to repeat what was already taught. To correct this frustrating situation, Jones advises: (1) the use of body language; (2) motivating by use of the incentive system; and (3) providing help to individual students.

Correct use of body language is extremely important and not a new concept. Natural teachers have employed it for years. It means carrying yourself with confidence as you breeze lightly and boldly to the front of the classroom, engaging all with direct eye contact. It means addressing the class heartily and with the stance of a determined and powerful figure. Most importantly, when teaching preschool, stay standing. If you sit down at the tables with the children, you lose your advantage of height. Little children in a group prefer to talk and play rather than listen to the teacher. Command their attention the way a captain does his crew, or the general his army. This is not autocracy. It is merely good theater. Little children love role models and the adult teacher is a powerful role model.

The incentive system has to be realistically devised to give the children what they want. In corporate America adults strive for raises, paid vacations, and holidays. But in preschool, what the children want above all else is approval, not necessarily praise, although that is good too. They crave to know that they're doing a good job, that their work is meeting the teacher's criteria, and that they are doing something the teacher thinks is worthwhile. Encouragement should come easily to the teacher's lips, and while praise is important, it should not be given indiscriminately. If the child "messes up," allow her to do the work over, provided this does not become a habit. Assumed inadequacy often rears its ugly head, and it is the task of the teacher to keep the child thinking positively about her work. Approval is the reward that keeps them coming back for more. If you occasionally say, "I think you all did such a good job today, I am going to give you stickers," that is an added incentive. Children love stickers and the teacher should always have them on hand; but again, use them sparingly. You don't want to rely too heavily on incentives. Stress that work is its own reward and that stickers are only for special occasions.

Helping individual students is a large part of the Jones model, which I have used successfully in my teaching. "Be positive, be brief, and be gone" is his advice. The children need daily feedback from the teacher in the form of encouragement and advice, but you should not do their work for them. I circulate about the classroom (we have two large tables with eight places each), and while the children are working, I make general remarks about what a good job they are doing, or I might talk a little more about the story. But when it comes time for them to say, "Excuse me, I'm ready for the four questions now," I go to each of them, and (this is very important) ask the same four questions: (1) "Did you draw a picture? (2) Did you color the picture? (3) Did you write a word (or a sentence)? (4) Did you write your name? If they answer "yes" to all these questions, they have successfully completed their journals for that day. Then I give my words of positive criticism. While they are working, I often make brief, constructive suggestions, especially if they cannot draw something or are having trouble with a concept.

As time goes by, and you become a more practiced teacher, you will be quick to notice the following things. Is the group paying attention? How was my entrance? Did I greet them positively and with joy? Are they glad to be here? Did I make sure they all had their shoes on and tied? Are they sitting in their own chairs with toys or extra clothes put under the chairs so that there are no distractions? Are they keeping hands and feet to themselves? Are they focused on my face and listening to my words, and am I speaking clearly enough? Loud enough? Slowly enough? Am I looking each of them in the eye as I let my gaze sweep the room? Most of all, do I love to be here, sharing my story with them? This private checklist comes automatically after a while and the beauty of discipline shows in the effective work of the children.

Giving a child an idea is another way to encourage right behavior. You may think that giving the class a whole story is enough, but this is not always the case. I had an extremely volatile four–year–old who lost his temper easily and got frustrated if things did not immediately go his way. And yet, he was also very quick and bright, and he was eager to journal because all his friends were doing it. When I told my story about the alligator that grew to monstrous proportions in a New York sewer pipe, he was enthralled, but when he tried to put his concepts down on paper, he became miserable because he could not draw anything. I knew if I challenged him with the right idea he would become focused. What do little boys notice the most about an alligator? Lots of sharp white teeth of terror and destruction. They like that. I approached the frustrated boy and asked, "What would you like to draw?" He replied, "An alligator." I drew one for him on the tent cardboard, and he tried without success to draw it. His face was turning red and he was getting frustrated. A hot, angry tear splashed onto the paper. "Wait a minute, Clem, I'll draw you something and you can finish what I start." So I took his red pen and drew big, white, zig–zaggy teeth on his paper. He was overjoyed. Alligator teeth! "You finish it!" I said. He not only finished it, but went on to color it bright crimson and orange. Then he wrote the word "alligator." He was beaming by the end of the class. What might have turned into a disaster and prevented him from coming back (journal class for four-year-olds is voluntary) was a triumph. He was eager for more.

Drawing, writing, journal-making are hard work. Reading is hard work. Most adults have forgotten how they struggled with that mysterious and demanding process when they were in first grade, and they have forgotten as well the disdain that classmates who could read had for those who could not. But go into any first grade class where reading is being taught, either by phonics, phonemes or the whole language method, and see the so-called bright kids who have "got it" and the sad, defeated, stumbling children who are trying their hardest to "get it," but aren't there yet. This is why I am so passionately devoted to teaching journaling in preschool. I want to give these children who falter every bit of help I can.

I stayed aware of Clem's short attention span, so I did not let him sit too long but kept my eye on him and hurried him through the transitions. He finished about 15 minutes before anyone else, but that was okay. I tried to tailor his efforts to the endurance he already possessed, and had confidence that with each succeeding journal class this endurance would grow.

"If you don't let boys cry real tears, they'll cry bullets," is a saying that applies to children like Clem. Already by age four he was violent, angry, and frustrated, and had a low sense of self-esteem. But he was full of talent too! I had to try to bring out his talents and make him feel good about doing the journal so he would feel good about himself and want to learn.

Another boy who was later diagnosed with attention deficit disorder was a violent child who did not respond well to correction. He had angry temper tantrums, tossed chairs about the room, and refused to talk to anybody. When he came to journal, I gave him the same story and pep talk that

I gave everyone else. He was calm and efficient throughout, enjoyed being with his peers and benefited from the structure and rules of doing the journal. This is one case where the automatic discipline already established in my journal class was a help to him. He was charming and did some wonderful pictures for his journal book.

If you get the children involved, there will be no discipline problems. When I tell my stories I often ask open-ended questions. The boys and girls love being called on, and at times it is difficult to get them to stop giving their answers. They get so excited they go on and on and sometimes the discussion goes off track. One will say, "I saw that movie!" and another will cry delightedly, "I saw it too. I own it!" and they start talking about the movie. If I'm not quick, my advantage as teacher is pulled out from under me. "That's very nice, but now we need to know what happened next in the story!" I bring them back to the subject in a polite but commanding voice. Then they listen.

One of the boys found a large odd-shaped rock in the playground one day, and I made a story about him and the rock, in which I said he had found a "dinosaur fossil." He glowed with pride. All the journal writers wanted to see his "fossil" and I let them use it as a prop.

Another time, I told the story of the cat with the question mark for a tail. Her owner first commands her to "Go catch the mice!" But the cat won't respond until he puts the words in the form of a question. He asks the cat politely, "Please, will you catch the mice?" Then I said, "The first time the owner *told* the cat what to do; the second time he *asked* her politely. Now turn to your neighbor and shake his hand. First *tell* him to let go, but then *ask* him politely and see the difference." Grinning, and a little shy, each child turned to his or her neighbor and shook hands. First, they told, then asked politely to be let go. It was fun. They got the idea to write "please" and "thank you" and "question mark" on their journal papers. Because they had shaken hands, this exercise in class involvement cemented them together in a brief expression of friendship that was very special. This is an example of positive discipline.

A calm, modulated voice is important in establishing and maintaining discipline. To ensure the best behavior on the part of the students, it is necessary for the teacher to keep control of his or her own emotions, to allow calmness and confidence come across in your voice. You can reserve a slightly sharper tone for sudden corrections, but don't let it become the norm. Calling the misbehaving child by name in just the right tone of voice is often all that is needed. You want class members to be working hard but keeping half an eye fixed on you, and not on their peers.

If children take interest in each other and not in the teacher, it becomes fun for them and a game to keep the teacher out. This is a very serious state of affairs and must be corrected at the outset. At the first sign that certain children are becoming leaders in disruption, you have to single them out and separate them. Divide and conquer. Do not let two volatile children or best friends sit next to one another. Put them at different tables, or even put one at an unused table. They will soon learn you mean business. If you are consistent in following this practice, you may not actually have to separate them but only say the words "If you don't settle down and stop talking to N—, I will invite you to sit at the white table." If the discipline is working, this will settle the child. If not, separate them.

Another form of group misbehavior that can cause a teacher trouble is buffoonery. This is very common among preschool children who would rather play and have fun with their peers than anything else. A teacher may be in the middle of telling a great story when the first one cries "Oooh," and suddenly they are all exclaiming "Ooooh" or "Aaaaah" or making other rude noises. They may have started doing this in response to the action of the story, but hearing all their friends doing it too makes it an irresistible game. I have found it useful to simply stop and face them silently for a minute. I then point out in a very respectful tone that I expect polite manners from them, and if they want me to continue telling the story, they must stop making unnecessary noises. Positive discipline.

There is much more to cover relating to discipline, but this book is not a behavioral management plan. I merely want to stress that without positive discipline, there can be no effective teaching. I repeat that discipline is not punishment. It is a two-way communication between teacher and students that requires respect on both sides. Democratic discipline depends on an agreement between teacher and student that certain rules are to be followed. These rules should be established at the beginning of the school year, and the class reminded of them from time to time to not forget what is expected. Children crave the security of structure, rules, order, and logical consequences. If the teacher provides these, he or she will have no trouble in teaching the group, and a new generation of would-be readers will be launched on their flight to literacy.

PART TWO

Easy Stories to Tell

1. A Birthday Present for Mom: The Color Red

A boy named Mike wanted to get his mother, the queen, a wonderful birthday present, but he didn't know what it should be. So he went for a walk in the woods where he met a magician. He recognized the magician because his clothes were covered with moons and stars, and he had a tall, peaked hat on his head and a wand in his hand. "What can I give my mother for her birthday?" he asked the magician. "Here is a tree. It's tall and green and beautiful. Give her a tree." But Mike answered him impatiently. "I can't give her a tree! I can't carry it. It's too big." So the magician waved his wand at the tree and instantly it was covered with small nuts called acorns. "There you have it! Give her acorns," said the magician. Mike was mad. "No," he shouted. "She's not a squirrel!" The magician waved his wand again and all the acorns disappeared. Gold coins appeared on the tree instead of leaves. "Give her money," he suggested. "She doesn't need money. She's a queen," said Mike. "Well, what's her favorite color?" the magician asked. "Red," answered the boy. "Then, look," cried the magician and waved his wand again at the tree. Instantly it turned from a money tree into one that was covered with bright red leaves. Under each leaf an apple peeked out rosy and ripe, red as could be. Mike was delighted. He climbed onto the magician's shoulders and picked the ripe, red apples. Then he took handfuls of the red leaves and put them in his pockets. "I need a basket," he said and the magician gave him a basket. He piled up the apples and leaves and took them to his mother, the queen. She was delighted and a wonderful smile came over her face. "How did you know my favorite color was red?" she asked as she ate a juicy red apple.

2. Mighty Mac and the Snowplow: A Birthday Story

A boy named Michael was going to have his sixth birthday. He invited all the children in his kindergarten class to come to his birthday party. "It will be fun!" he told them. "I will have a cake and ice cream. Everyone will get a brightly colored balloon, and we will play games like Pin the Tail on the Donkey and Twister. Please come." The children were happy to be invited. They couldn't wait to go to Michael's party! But on the day of his birthday, there was a big snowstorm. So much snow fell that it was hard to open the doors of the houses to go outside. Michael was sad and went to tell his dad. "I am afraid I cannot have my party. There is too much snow. The cars cannot drive on the roads." But Michael's dad was known as "Mighty Mac" in the town because he drove a big snowplow. He put on his snowpants, his boots, his jacket and his hat. He went out to get his snowplow and turned on the engine. "Rooaar!" went the snowplow. Mighty Mac was off! He drove down one street after another clearing the snow away. Soon there was plenty of space for the cars to drive on. All Michael's friends got into their cars with their parents and came to Michael's party. This made Michael very happy, but happiest of all was Mighty Mac, because he knew that he and his big snowplow had saved Michael's party.

GR

GRANDMOTHER

AND THE G

KATIE

3. Jack's Family: A Family Theme

Once there was a boy named Jack who was five years old. He lived with his mom and dad and was happy because he had his own room with lots of toys and a pet dog to play with. One day Mom and Dad called to him and asked him if he would like to have a new little baby brother or sister. "Yes," said Jack. "That would be fun." But after a few months, when his mom brought a new baby sister home from the hospital, Jack did not find it to be much fun. The baby took all of Mom's attention, it seemed. All she did was cry and drink milk, and when she wasn't crying, she slept. Everyone held her and made a fuss over her. It seemed to Jack that no one paid any attention to him anymore. He was very sad, and because he was so sad, he forgot to feed his dog. When he accidentally knocked over the water dish, he did not mop up the water with a towel. "Jack!" said his dad in an angry voice. "Mop up that water!" He did it, but he was angry too. Jack's mom knew something was troubling him. She called him to her and gave him a big hug. "What's the matter, Jack? Don't you like your new baby sister?" Jack was truthful. "No," he said. "I don't like her at all. All she does is eat and sleep and cry, and everyone makes a fuss over her." Mom gave Jack another hug. "It won't always be like this," she said. "It is only because she is very small that your sister cannot play with you. She will grow fast and when she gets bigger she will play with you and be your friend. We are a family, Jack. We all love each other. We want you to love your baby sister as much as you love us, your mom and dad." Jack thought about it. Then he asked to do something he had never done before. He asked to hold his baby sister. Mom told him to sit down and she put the baby in his lap. He saw how cute she was. "You will grow up someday," he said. "Soon!" said Mom. "In only a year or two, she will walk and talk, and you will be friends."

The four
brown
butterflies
turned yellow.
Matthew

4. Wheels: An Expository Story

J ames was riding on his skateboard. "Whee!" he shouted as he went very fast down the street. He was going so fast that he nearly ran over his cat, and then he almost tripped the mailman. He was going so fast the wind sang in his ears and his mouth opened wide to breathe it all in. He almost forgot to watch where he was going. "Hold on, young fella," said the mailman. "Slow down before you run over someone on your wheels." James slowed and jumped off his skateboard. "I can go faster than the wind!" he said. "Your wheels can do that," replied the mailman. "But did you know there was a time long ago when there were no wheels?" James was startled. "No wheels?" he asked in surprise. "How did the cars get around?" The mailman smiled. "There were no cars. There was nothing that traveled on wheels. There were no trains, no buses, no bicycles. There were no skateboards, no airplanes, no tricycles, no motorcycles." James was puzzled. "What did the people use to get around? How did they move things from place to place?" he asked. The mailman said, "They had horses to ride, but travel was much slower without wheels. They hauled things up and down ramps by hitching ropes to them and pulling them by hand. It was hard, heavy work. People had to lift and carry heavy objects, but they couldn't move them very far. One day someone invented a wheel—an axle with two round stones at each end. Then they learned how to bend wood and make wooden wheels. Finally they learned how to make wheels of steel and rubber. It became possible to travel far distances and to build great cities. Trains and planes and automobiles, as well as your skateboard became possible. Wheels were among the most wonderful inventions to happen to mankind. I hope you appreciate them now." Jack picked up his skateboard and put it down again after spinning its four wheels. "Yes, I do!" he said. "Now I know that there wasn't always an invention called the wheel, I appreciate wheels and my skateboard more than ever!"

5. The Bubbles That Wouldn't Break: The Letter "B"

Once there was a boy named Ted who was having a birthday party. As a special surprise, his mom invited a magician to perform tricks for him. The magician handed Ted some bubble soap and waved his magic wand. "Abracadabra! Now you will have bubbles that won't break!" Ted couldn't wait to try his new bubble soap. He blew bubbles all around the room and not a single one broke. He tried touching them with his fingers, pressing them against the walls, and stepping on them, but still they would not break. There were so many bubbles that they floated up to the ceiling and pushed the roof off. Then they floated in bouncing rainbows of color up into the sky and scared a flock of birds. Ted got a telescope and watched to see how high his bubbles would go. He saw them float into the atmosphere, the stratosphere, and the ionosphere until they were out of sight. They floated up past the moon and kept floating until they landed on the planet Mars. On Mars, the Martians were getting ready to invade Earth. They saw the bubbles that wouldn't break and knew they came from an Earthling. They tried and tried to break the bubbles but could not. Finally, they said, "We cannot break these Earth bubbles. That means the Earthlings are too strong for us! We better not invade Earth. If Ted had been able to hear them, he would have known that his bubbles had saved the planet.

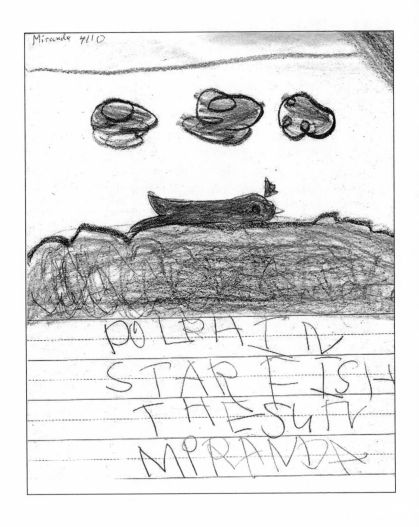

DOLPHIN
STARFISH
THE SUN
MIRANDA

6. The Red Balloon: The Letter "B" and the Color Red

Once there were three balloons at a child's birthday party—a red one, a yellow one, and a blue one. They were filled with helium instead of air so they floated up high on the end of their strings. Suddenly, a gust of wind came and carried the balloons away on the breeze, they moved higher and higher until they looked like three dark dots against the sun. Blue Balloon floated over skyscrapers in the city and got caught in a downdraft. He smashed into a tall building and broke into a thousand pieces. Yellow Balloon took off on the wind and was swept out to sea over the masts of sailboats and the smokestacks of steamers. He went farther and farther away and finally he disappeared where sea and sky meet. But Red Balloon wanted to stay close to earth and find a child who would play with her. Although the wind was pushing her, she tried to dive down to greet some children in a playground. Some big, rough boys were playing basketball. "Oh look! A red balloon! Let's catch it!" they cried, and jumped as high as they could, reaching for her string, but they were not the kind of friends Red Balloon was seeking. She sailed away from them and over little houses with neat backyards. She saw a spot of red coming closer. It was a pretty red dress on a little girl who sat on the grass crying for her mother. "I want my mommy! Oh, where is she? When will she come back from the store?" Red Balloon floated gently down and landed with a bump on the grass right next to the little girl. "Oh! How wonderful! A red balloon just for me." She smiled and began to laugh. Red Balloon felt very happy because she had made the little girl laugh, and she lived with her for a long time ever after.

7. Boy Scouts Find the Treasure: The Letter "M"

Once there were two boy scouts who wanted to go camping. They got all their gear together and went into the woods and set up camp at the bottom of Mad Mountain. It was called Mad Mountain because there was a secret treasure hidden in it, but no one had been able to find it, and so these disappointed searchers got mad! Mike and Matthew, the two boy scouts, knew they could find the treasure if they only had a map. They set their tents up, took out their axes, and began to chop trees down to get firewood. In one of the trees there was a hole. Excited by their discovery, they reached into the hole and took out a metal box. They opened it to discover a treasure map. It had a picture of the tree where their camping place was, and a trail marked in red ink that went past an elephant–shaped rock, past a lake with an island in it, and up a rockslide to Mad Mountain. There was an X showing the treasure. Mike and Matthew set out to follow the map. They went past the elephant–shaped rock, and past the lake with the island, and finally up the rockslide. There they found a dark hole in the side of the hill. "A cave!" cried Matthew. "That must be where the treasure is hidden." Mike picked up two sticks and beat them together with a loud sound. "I am scaring the bear out of the cave so we can go in it," he said. Soon a very angry black bear came out. "Quick! Up a tree!" yelled Mike to Matthew. The two boys climbed a tree fast as lightning. The bear growled and walked all around the tree, but after awhile it went away. The boy scouts climbed down and went inside the cave. They shone their flashlights on old rock walls until they found a crack in the stone. Inside the crack was another metal box, just like the first one. They were excited! They took it outside the cave and a safe distance away before they opened it. It had a treasure inside all right, chocolate M & M's candy!

8. Herman the Mouse Goes to the Moon: The Letter "M"

Herman the mouse lived in Cape Canaveral where rockets are launched to go to the moon. He always wanted to go to the moon because when he looked up at the sky on a hot summer night, it looked exactly as if it were made of green cheese. One day he sneaked aboard a rocket ship. It blasted off and carried Herman the mouse and three astronauts through space. Finally they landed on the moon and got out of the rocket and walked around. The astronauts were wearing pressurized suits that had air tanks fastened to their backs with hoses connecting oxygen to their helmets so they could breathe. But poor Herman! He had no suit and no helmet. Worst of all, he had no air tanks. There was no air on the moon. He discovered that it was not made of green cheese, but only hard, white moon rocks. Herman gasped and tried to breathe. An astronaut saw him and put him inside his helmet so he could share the oxygen. Then they picked up some moon rocks to take as souvenirs. Then they all climbed back into the rocket ship and blasted off for Earth. No one was gladder to get home than Herman the mouse.

koalabear
eucalyptus
tree
thebout

9. Sugar Bear: The Letter "S"

They called him "Sugar Bear" because he longed for anything sweet. Sugar Bear was a medium–sized brown bear, who lived with his mom and dad in the woods. He ate nuts, roots, grubs, berries, but he was always hungry for something new. One day he went for a long walk in a search for food and he came to the edge of the forest where a little girl, Sarah, lived with her parents. Sarah was playing in the yard when she saw Sugar Bear. "Oh! Hello brown bear!" she said in a friendly fashion, for she had never been taught to be afraid of bears. "Are you hungry? Well, don't eat me! I'll give you something better to eat!" And she went into the house and came out with a chocolate chip cookie, which she gave to the bear. It was so full of sugar and so delightfully sweet that Sugar Bear was very happy. He did somersaults and leaped in the air!

The next day, he came back again. Sarah gave him a pancake dripping with maple syrup. Sugar Bear jumped for joy. The third day, he was back again. Sarah gave him a honeycomb filled with golden wild–bee honey. But Sarah's mother saw her feeding the bear and was very frightened. When Sarah came into the house, her mother scolded her. "Sarah! Don't encourage that bear. You've got to stop feeding him because I want him to stay far away from our home." Sarah was very sad, but she was an obedient child and did what her mother said. When the bear came back, she held up her hands and shooed him away. "I can't feed you any more. Mom says you have to go away from here," Sarah said sadly. Sugar Bear was sad too, but he went.

One day much later in the summer, Sarah was out in the forest picking blueberries, when she lost her way and couldn't find the path home. The trees all looked alike and the path she was following turned into another path which suddenly disappeared. Sarah threw herself down on the cold forest floor and began to cry. Suddenly a warm, soft nose touched her cheek. She blinked the tears from her eyes and saw her friend, Sugar Bear, standing over her. She flung her arms around his furry neck. "Oh help me! Help me, Sugar Bear!" she cried. "I've been lost for such a long time and I am so hungry!" So Sugar Bear took Sarah to his cave and offered her the best he had, tasty nuts and yummy roots, and fresh, juicy berries. She was happy eating his food.

Sarah lived with Sugar Bear for two weeks, until one day, she heard her name called when playing outside his cave. "Sarah! Sarah!" called her dad. He was coming up the hill! Sarah ran to him and hugged him with all her might. She told him how Sugar Bear found her when she was lost and fed her nuts, roots and berries. Dad was so pleased with the big brown bear that he smiled broadly. "Why Sugar Bear! You saved Sarah's life. You are welcome to come to our house anytime and eat chocolate chip cookies, heaps of pancakes with sweet sticky maple syrup and honeycomb with lots of golden honey—and no bees!"

10. One Feather, Native American Boy: The Letter "F"

One Feather was a Native American boy who had only one feather in his headdress. He longed to have many feathers like his father, the chief, who was stern and strong and told all the people in the tribe what to do. "What can I do to become a chief like you?" One Feather asked his father one day. The chief answered. "You must be brave and strong. You must go on a long journey and find the black fox with a white-tipped tail and ask him for one of his whiskers. When you come back, I will know you are strong enough to be a chief and I will give you many feathers for your headdress." One Feather set out on his journey. He climbed mountains and crossed rivers. He grew hungry and thirsty. But he always found something to eat, and along the way, he learned to talk to animals. One day, he met a black bear. "What do you want?" growled the bear. One Feather knew how to talk to the bear and he growled back, "Can you tell me how to get to the fox with his white-tipped tail?" The bear answered him, "The fox lives in a cave at the top of this mountain." One Feather began to climb the mountain. As he tripped over some loose rocks, a rattlesnake reared up before him on the path, shaking its rattle. "Who dares to disturb me? I am rattling my tail to warn you that I will bite you with my poison and you will die." One Feather was not afraid. He knew how to talk to the rattlesnake. "Please, good snake, I did not mean to harm you. I only want to find the cave with the black fox." The snake replied. "He is out hunting. Wait by the cave until he returns." So One Feather waited until the sun crossed the sky at noon and began to sink into the West. Just as its rays were turning red, he saw the fox. He leaped upon him and hugged his neck. "Please give me a whisker so I can be chief," he pleaded. The fox struggled and cried out, "Let go of me. You can have your whisker." He let One Feather pluck out the whisker and then ran into the cave. One Feather was delighted! He traveled as fast as he could back to the village of the chief and gave his father the feather. In a big ceremony, One Feather was given a headdress of many eagle feathers that fell to his knees, and he became chief when his father died.

11. The Magic Grandmother and the Butterfly: The Letter "N"

Here is a picture of a clock. See the hands pointing to the numbers? That tells what time it is. When the two hands of the clock are both pointing straight up at the number twelve, it is noon during the day. One day, a little girl named Sarah was playing outside in her backyard when the hands of the clock were almost pointing to noon. She was having a wonderful time chasing butterflies. It was a sunny day and the butterflies all gleamed with pretty colors—orange, blue, yellow, and brown with purple spots. Sarah tried catching them with her hands, but as soon as she ran to the butterflies, they flew high out of her reach. Her grandmother was sitting nearby. "Why don't you try a butterfly net?" she asked and showed Sarah the long–handled stick with a soft green net on the end to form a sack. "It won't hurt them and you can let them go after you catch them. Just be very quiet and sneak up on them." Sarah tried to be quiet but it was hard for her because she loved to shout when she caught a butterfly. Every time she crept up on one, she would shout "I've got you!" and the butterfly would escape. Finally, all the bright colored butterflies had flown away. Only a large brown one remained. She sneaked up behind him and this time did not shout when she lowered the net over him. He was caught! She brought the brown butterfly back to her grandmother but it was such a plain, ugly butterfly that she began to cry.

"Don't be sad because your butterfly is only brown and not brightly colored," said Grandma. "If you love him, you can do magic to him. Here! Like this." She passed her hands over the net with the brown butterfly inside it. Nothing seemed to happen. "Did you love him?" Grandma asked. "No, not enough," Sarah replied. "I'll tell you what to do," Grandma said. "Close your eyes and love him very much, and then, exactly at noon let him free to fly up into the sun. You will see a wonderful sight." Sarah did as Grandma told her. She closed her eyes and loved that butterfly as hard as she could, and when she opened them, it was noon. She shook out the net and sent the butterfly flying up into the blue sky. Suddenly he turned from brown to the most wonderful color gold, for he was a magic butterfly. All she needed to do was to love him as much as she loved her grandmother.

12. Roger Learns to Have a Heart: The Letter "H"

Roger went with his mom and dad to the pet store where there were some very cute puppies climbing over one another, trying to lick his hand. He petted them happily. "Will you buy me a puppy?" he asked. "We don't know if we can right now," said his parents. "You have to have a heart to care for a puppy, to feed him, to give him water, to take him for walks, and to train him to be a good dog." Roger did not know what it meant when his parents said he needed to have a heart. He already had one inside his chest and he could feel it beating every day. Couldn't his mom and dad see that? But that is not what they meant. When Roger went to his preschool, he was the kind of boy who always waited till his friends built a block tower. Then he would rush in on them and knock it down, and laugh at them. (Was that being a nice friend? No!) When they went out to the playground, his friends tried to dig in the sand, but Roger would tip over their buckets and then throw sand at them. (Was that being a nice friend? No!) When they had inside play, he would take away his friend's Matchbox trucks and hide them. (Was that being a nice friend? Certainly not!) His teacher told his mom and dad, "I'm afraid Roger has not got a heart. He is not kind to his friends. He does not play nicely with them, and he does not share." Roger's parents were very sad when they heard this. "We certainly can't get you a puppy to love and care for if you cannot even play nicely with your preschool friends," they said. "When will you learn to have a heart?" Roger thought about it. "What about tomorrow?" he said. "I'll be a good friend. I'll share, and you will see that I have a heart." The next day he helped his friends build a tower of blocks instead of knocking it down. He even stopped other children from knocking it down. In the playground, he was careful not to throw sand, and he helped to fill the buckets. Inside, he did not snatch away anyone's Matchbox trucks. He even brought his own Beast Wars action figure into school to share. "Roger has been doing wonderful today," said his teacher to his mom and dad. "He's playing nicely with his friends and sharing. I think he's learned what it means to have a heart." Then Mom and Dad went right out and bought Roger the puppy.

13. Turtle Tries to Find a Neck:
The Letter "N"

Once there was a turtle who was not happy with his neck. He wandered down to the pond and met a frog. "I wish I had your neck," he said to the frog. "It's so good looking because it blends in so smoothly with your head and is such a pretty, shiny, green color." But the frog just laughed at the turtle. "My neck only lets me look straight ahead because I cannot turn it from side to side. Your neck is better. You should be happy with your neck." But Turtle was not happy, and he walked on until he heard an owl hooting from the top of a tall tree. Turtle craned his neck and looked up at the owl who blinked and seemed to turn his head all the way around. "I wish I had your neck," said Turtle. "You can turn your head right around on it." But Owl said, "No I can't. It only looks that way. Your neck is better because you can look up. I can't." Then he flew away. Turtle still did not like his neck. He walked on until he met a giraffe. He stopped and stared in wonder at the giraffe's long neck, tall as the tallest tree. Turtle's mouth hung open in amazement. "I wish I had your neck," he said. "You can reach to the top of the trees. My neck is so short compared to yours that I could just cry," and a big tear welled up in his eye and dropped onto the grass. "Don't cry about your neck," said the giraffe kindly. "It may be shorter than mine, but it lets you move freely and drink water easily. I have to bend my knees and lower my whole neck down to the ground just to get a drink. Don't I look silly?" He did look silly as he tried to drink from the pond, but Turtle still wasn't happy with his short neck. He wished he had a neck like Frog's, or Owl's, or Giraffe's. Then he met a monkey, swinging from the trees over his head. "Your neck can do everything mine can do," said the monkey. "You can look up to the sky or down to the ground. You can look from side to side. And best of all, your neck can do something that I wish mine could do, but I can't." The turtle wanted to know. "What can my neck do that yours can't?" he asked. "You can pull it right into your shell and hide your head from danger," said the monkey. "No wild animal could ever eat you once you have pulled your head and neck into your shell. But I have to run for my life!" Turtle thought about this and pulled his head inside his shell just for practice. It was warm and dark and safe in there. He decided then that he liked his neck after all, and he never complained about it again.

14. The Grim Giant: The Letter "G"

Once there was a giant who never laughed. He did not even smile, but went around being grouchy about things that happened to him every day. For this reason everyone in the town called him "The Grim Giant" and stayed out of his way for fear he would stomp on them. The Grim Giant told the people in the town that there was to be no singing and no laughing, and above all, the children must never play happy games. This made all the townspeople very sad but they could do nothing about it because he was a giant. One day he went away on a trip, and while he was gone the children laughed and played. Oh, how they loved to laugh after such a long, gloomy time of being quiet! All too soon the Grim Giant came back. They could hear the stump, stump, stump of his heavy boots as he came over the hills. At the same time, a juggler named Griswold was passing through town. He was juggling three gold balls in the air to make the children laugh. When they heard the giant coming, the people were afraid Griswold would leave them. "Oh please stay and juggle your balls and try to make the giant laugh," they cried, "for once he has started laughing, he will feel how good it is and he will not be grim any longer." Griswold looked up at the huge giant coming over the hills. He was brave and strong. "I'll try my best," he said. The Grim Giant saw Griswold tossing three gold balls in the air, but he did not laugh. "What are you doing? Get out of here!" he roared. Griswold looked up at him and smiled. "I am trying to make you laugh. Will this make you laugh?" and he began to juggle a spoon, a fork, and a knife, but still the giant did not laugh. Griswold dropped the spoon and fork and knife, and picked up the castle butler sitting on a chair. Then he picked up the sword carrier standing at attention. Also, he picked up the cook and the pot she was holding. He juggled them high in the air and brought them safely down again. The giant laughed and laughed. He laughed so hard the castle walls shook. He forgot all about being grim and rolled on the ground, still laughing. "You can stay here and juggle for me every day," he told Griswold when he had finally got his breath, "and the children can play, sing, and laugh and have their games again." Griswold and all the people were delighted! The juggler stayed in town and juggled for the giant, the children, and the townspeople every day. They gave him a nice house in town and a roast beef dinner every Sunday. He juggled at all the great feasts in the castle and everyone was happy, but the butler, the sword carrier, and the cook were careful to stay out of his way because they could never get used to being juggled!

PART THREE

Book Making

The Crown of Achievement

L ucky children have books in their lives from an early age. At our preschool, toddlers of 18 months old are surrounded by books. Even these very little children love to thumb through the pages, look at the pictures, and guess at the meaning of the stories printed there. They develop a fierce affection for their favorite books and yearn to be able to decipher the mysteries of the written words. That is why the crowning achievement of the journal class is to produce, four times during the year, a book by each student—one that they can read because they have written it. There is nothing more exciting to the children at the end of each quarter when I hand out their completed books—pages of their writings and drawings enclosed in a cover of their own making. The boys and girls fall upon their books with glad cries as they savor again each story and compare their work to that of their friends. It is a very rewarding moment for the students and teacher alike.

Memory is a vital part of reading. Without the ability to retain what has been read, one cannot understand any but the briefest piece of writing. Therefore, the building of memory skills is an important step in learning to read. Because of the dynamic nature of the journal teaching method, when the children see their completed journal books, they easily recall the entire story with great accuracy. This helps them remember the words they have written and the title of the story (or salient theme) I have placed at the bottom of each page. I encourage them to go over the books with their parents, and it is with a sense of pride that they take their books home to be read and reread.

Parents have come up to me and said that their children were making their own journal books at home and asked for special paper to create them. One parent told me that his son, who was in second grade, was writing a whole book and had finished two chapters of it, "all because of your journal class." Such feedback is wonderful to hear. But even for the children who do not achieve such heights, the foundation of connecting words to pictures will aid them when they begin to read in first grade. From the evidence and feedback from parents and students, journal writing has the effect for which it was designed—the successful teaching of pre-reading and pre-writing skills.

The making of book covers is always an exciting event that the children look forward to wholeheartedly. We use ordinary construction paper folded in half to fit 8 1/2 x 11 inch journal paper. These sheets are folded on the left so that children do not make their covers upside down. (I warn them that if they move the covers, the fold must always be on the left.) Then I tell a story with a cover for a theme. I pass out red pens, black pens, pencils, markers, and crayons, and instruct the class to draw themes from the story or other ideas that they particularly enjoy. On the chalkboard I draw a variety of popular pictures, rainbows, flowers, unicorns, race cars—anything they might be interested in drawing. They get to work with enthusiasm.

Fifteen minutes before the end of the class, I hand out stickers, lots of stickers. There is an art to using stickers in an interesting way, and some children are very skillful at creating patterns. When these colorful covers are finished, I collect them and take them home. That night, from each child's file folder, I take all the drawings from the quarter and staple them with three or four staples along the edge of the fold. I also include a letter to parents explaining each step of journal writing. Samples of these letters are included in the appendix.

The next day, I take the finished books back to school and pass them out. If it is the fourth quarter of the year and the kindergarten class is graduating, I make an additional certificate of excellence. This resembles a diploma with a few words of approval and a drawing. I make one master diploma, copy it on the copy machine, then write each child's name as a special mark of esteem. The smiles and grins are as abundant as sunshine when the diplomas are passed out.

Following is an example of a cover story. It is a complex one that the children love, and it is given at the end of the school year when their faculties have been honed by a year of journal writing.

Rustem Makes a Cover

In faraway Arabia a prince named Rustem went with his teacher, Ahmed, and they roamed about woods and fields. Ahmed the teacher would tell stories about the wonders of nature, the birds that sang, the sun that came up each day and hurried down into the sea each night, how it brought heat and life to the world by day, and how the darkness and cool air ruled the night when moon and stars were the only light. The prince was eager to learn the habits of all the animals of the forest. Prince Rustem was so enchanted with the stories and the things he had learned that he went home and asked for paper. On this paper, he drew pictures of the wondrous things he had seen, and wrote wonderful words to describe them. "Congratulations, Prince Rustem, you have made a journal book," said Ahmed, his teacher. Rustem was pleased. "I would like to present it as a gift to the sultan, my father," he said. "Then you will need a cover, something strong to protect your words," said Ahmed. "Go forth and find materials to make one!"

So Rustem mounted his favorite horse and rode away looking for a cover for his wonderful book. First, he went into the forest and found a tree. "I will make my cover out of wood!" he cried and got out his axe. But before he could strike the first blow, the tree called out, "Rustem! Rustem! Don't slay me!" So Rustem did not cut down the tree.

Then he went into the market place where he saw some women weaving red cloth. "I will make my cover of cloth!" he said, but when he picked up the cloth, it cried out in a loud voice "Spare me! For I'm not strong enough to make a cover for your book." Rustem got back on his horse and rode out into the country where some cows were at pasture in the green field. He looked at their strong hides and said, "I will make my cover out of cowhide!" And again he picked up his axe to slay the cow. "But I plead to you for mercy!" cried the cow. "Don't kill me. I need to stay alive to give you milk for your breakfast each morning." Rustem did not want to go without milk, so he did not slay the cow.

Now he did not know what to do. So, he went to his grandmother's house and sat beside the fire in her warm kitchen, feeling sad. "What's bothering you?" she asked. "I drew and colored and wrote a wonderful book, a journal book," replied Rustem. "I want to present it to my father the Sultan as a wondrous gift. But I need a cover: not wood, not cloth, not cowhide. What can I do?' Now his grandmother was very wise. She had saved from her birthday party the purple paper that she had used to make decorations. She held it out to Rustem. "Now fold this to the right size and decorate it with markers and crayons and stickers. It will be your cover," she said. Rustem was overjoyed. He decorated it beautifully and gave it to his father. The sultan was so pleased he made a gift to Rustem of all the horses in his stable and half his kingdom.

APPENDIX

Letters to Parents

About Letters to Parents

The letters that follow are intended for teachers to give to parents after the completion of each of four journals. Parents need reminders that their approval is the major impetus to enhancing learning skills, as well as imprinting what has been learned. Encourage them to take time to read over their child's journals and enjoy their drawings. With such cooperation at home, children become eager to take the next steps toward literacy.

DEAR PARENTS

Your son or daughter has been working hard at writing and drawing since September. In this journal, you see the results of what was both play and work. The pictures may look deceptively simple, but much learning and skill–building went into their making. First the children had to listen attentively and remember a story I told. They had to conceptualize some aspect of it and draw that conceptualization on the page using fine motor skills with pencil, crayon, or magic marker. Then they had to write a word or words copied from my writing. And finally, they confirmed their sense of possession of the work they had done by writing their names.

Many of these children are preliterate and are just learning their letters. They need to practice daily. The journal writing class gives them an opportunity to develop writing and prereading skills in preparation for the more difficult work they will undertake in the upper grades. Don't forget that such professionals as artists, mathematicians, engineers, and astronomers began their work by conceptualizing and then putting ideas on paper.

So too did your child work to putting ideas on paper, bringing his or her best to this task and producing these enchanting images. I ask you to look at the pages in this journal book carefully and go over them with your child. Your interest contributes to the learning process. As your child continues to draw and write in the journal each day, he or she will be thinking of your reactions. Your enthusiasm will inspire a deeper commitment to develop more journal skills.

Xo

On the Completion of Journal Book Two

DEAR PARENTS

Your son or daughter has been working hard to complete this second journal book. The children have shown increased attention and memory skills as they listened to the oral presentation of stories. By discovering a predominate theme, they have shown ability in logical constructive thought.

When they seize the most colorful and exciting moment of the story to use in their drawings, they are expressing those moments of inner experience that are meaningful to them. Using the tools of pencil, crayon, gel pens or markers, the children find satisfaction in drawings that mirror their creative drives. They also learn basic math concepts by using space and ratio, placement of objects on the page, how they relate to each other, size concepts of large to small, diminishment to enlargement, and proportion. Drawing is crucial to prepare for many subjects of higher education.

In journal class we explore the world of letters and numbers, science and fantasy. We learn the principles of Gauss' Law, how lighting strikes, and how negative and positive ions war with each other in a thundercloud. We learn about antigravity when a princess laughs so that she floats above the trees and cannot get down until the court magician saddens her at the sight of a poor donkey. In another tale we learn the qualities of a true princess, how she is so tender that she will be bruised even though there are seven mattresses between her and a tiny pea. We then discuss her noble character. This leads to open-ended questions about what is noble character, which leads to the next tale about a knight who is asked by an angry populace to kill a dragon with whom he shares poems and tea.

The children give their opinions and participate in class discussions that stimulate imaginative faculties and enhance writing abilities. They compose their own sentences about the pictures they have drawn. After pondering their artwork, they speak out their ideas, which I write for them to copy. This approach cultivates reading skills: first they see, then they hear the words, and then they write.

Your child is proud of learning to read and will often take sentences home and read them over again. You can encourage this new skill by listening as your son or daughter reads the words that accompany their pictures in Journal Book Two.

DEAR PARENTS

This third journal book shows how much your child has improved since September. Class time is very demanding. The children must pay attention to a story and then select ideas from the story from which to draw a picture (conceptualize). Then they color using three or more colors, sometimes creating backgrounds or outlines to enhance their figures. We learn to explore the complementary color principle, use of light and dark, contrasting colors, and the rainbow effect. Color as differentiation is an important idea that promotes sharp observation and definition of thought patterns.

The use of words is just as important to the process as drawing and coloring. Words as description come first, and then words become tools to explore the four basic kinds of sentences: declarative, exclamatory, the question, and the quotation. The five-part process—listening to the story, drawing from the story, coloring the drawing, selecting the appropriate words to accompany the drawing, and then writing the words—is done in a 45-minute time period of intense concentration. The triumph of signing one's name contributes to a sense of satisfaction and self worth. By the end of this task, your child is ready for a rest!

Imagine the same circumstance for yourselves if you were told to listen attentively to a complex story never heard before, and then asked to draw a picture of the features that loomed largest in your mind. Now imagine the fertile mind of a child trying to grasp some of these ideas and draw with much less skill while learning how to use a pencil and hold a crayon.

I teach the children how to draw with geometric shapes, and how to bear down hard on crayons to get good colors. I encourage them to put something down on paper just to get going, even if just a zig-zag or a squiggle. Each child must come up with original words or sentences. These visual and writing skills do not come easily, but must be developed through daily routines of consistent practice and effort, with an element of fun thrown in. It is up to the teacher *and parents* to keep children eager to learn. Join with me in congratulating your child's accomplishments.

On the Completion of Four Journal Books

DEAR PARENTS

Congratulations! Your child has now completed four journal books of writing, drawing and coloring. Since September the class has come a long way and you must be very proud! Children who began the year drawing exploratory scribbles now complete drawings of significance and depth. From the tentative use of one or two colors, they have come to embrace the entire spectrum and use crayons vigorously, covering the whole page with a palette as varied as those of Renoir or Monet. I am not exaggerating! Feast your eyes on the colorful drawings in these pages. And notice the writing. From a few, carefully penned letters, the children have expanded their skills into writing full words, with each word matched to a concept in the accompanying picture. Some have even ventured into the realm of descriptive sentences.

A lot of work has gone into making these books—a lot of thought, conceptualizing and writer's cramp from trying so hard. Once children learn that the daily effort applied to a journal page is an ongoing exercise, they are better prepared for the rigors of first grade. And once they experience the satisfaction of getting it down on paper, they begin to enjoy their effort and appreciate its importance. It has been my aim to instill an appetite for hard work of the kind that gets results.

I hope you keep this concept of success firmly in mind when you look over this journal with your child. Your enthusiasm is the best encouragement you can give, and ensures continuing commitment and confidence throughout the higher grades. I commend and salute our young journal writers and wish every success with the challenges to be met in the years ahead.

Xo

Sources

Applestein, Charles D. "A Typical Time-Out-Progression." *No Such Thing As A Bad Kid.* Gifford School of Weston, MA, 1998.

Charles, C.M. "The Jones Model." *Building Classroom Discipline.* New York: Longman, 1982.

Ibid. "The Dreikurs Model."

Dinesen, Isak. "Of Hidden Thoughts And Of Heaven." *Last Tales.* Random House, 1975.

Ibid. "The Blank Page."

Brown, Margaret Wise and Cooney, Barbara, eds. *Read Me Another Story.* New York: Thomas J. Crowell Co., 1948.

Hamilton, Edith. *Mythology, a Mentor Book.* The New American Library, 1942.

Hoffman, Daniel. "Edgar Allen Poe on Unity Of Effect." *Poe, Poe, Poe, Poe, Poe, Poe, Poe.* The Louisiana State University Press, 1972.

Jalongo, Mary Renck. "Teaching Young Children To Become Better Listeners," *National Association for the Education of Young Children Journal,* 1994.

McGuiness, Diane. *Why Our Children Can't Read And What We Can Do About It.* Simon and Schuster, 1997.

Nelsen, Jane. "Four Mistaken Goals Of Behavior." *Positive Discipline.* New York: Ballantine Books, 1987.

Ibid. "The Isolation Technique."

Ibid. "The Positive Approach."

Walley, Dean, and Bakes, Cindy. *A Funny Cake.* Hallmark and Stanford University Preschool Program.

About the Author

Margaret B. King has taught reading for twelve years, beginning as a teacher's assistant to the elementary grades at Derry Village School, in Derry New Hampshire. For six years at this school, she taught poor readers and gifted children by the means of phonics, phonemes, and textual definition. Since then she has taught at The Perfect Place for Children in Pelham, New Hampshire. At this school she formulated her method based on picture–word association, fine motor control, drawing for spatial definition, coloring as categorization, letter and word recognition, sounding out phonemes, and copying letters from left to right. In addition, she taught remedial reading under the government sponsored program, English As A Second Language.

King has a liberal arts degree from Boston College (1969) and a certificate in early childhood education (1995) from the University of New Hampshire. For postgraduate work she attended the University of Maine for courses in primary school education. In addition, she studied fine art at the Universidad de las Americas in Mexico City and at the prestigious Skowhegan School of Painting and Sculpture in Skowhegan, Maine. A practising artist for 17 years, she exhibited her work in galleries on the North Shore of Massachusetts, hosting several one–person shows.

Although King enjoyed practising and teaching art (at Masconomet Regional High School, Lyman School for Boys, and Park Private School in Massachusetts), she gravitated toward educating young children because of their spontaneous and inspiring minds. The use of her vivid imagination for painting was the springboard for learning how to teach reading by the methods presented in *Tadpole Tales*. This book is the culmination of years of dedicated and inspired teaching.